Finding Happiness in a Complex World

Charles P. Nemeth, JD, PhD, LLM

Finding Happiness in a Complex World

Rules from Aristotle and Aquinas

SOPHIA INSTITUTE PRESS
Manchester, New Hampshire

Finding Happiness in a Complex World was originally published by Anthem Press, London, in 2020, under the title *Living in Happiness in a Complex World.*

Material used in the first chapter of this work is excerpted from Charles P. Nemeth's *A Comparative Analysis of Cicero and Aquinas: Nature and the Natural Law,* published by Bloomsbury Academic, 2017.

Cover design by LUCAS Art & Design, Jenison, MI.

On the cover: painting of St. Thomas Aquinas (ca. 1400) by Gentile da Fabriano; Aristotle at his writing desk, image from a medieval manuscript (1457); images courtesy of Wikimedia Commons and in the public domain.

Unless otherwise noted, Scripture references in this book are taken from the Douay-Rheims edition of the Old and New Testaments. All emphases added.

Sophia Institute Press
Box 5284, Manchester, NH 03108
1-800-888-9344
www.SophiaInstitute.com

Sophia Institute Press is a registered trademark of Sophia Institute.

paperback ISBN 978-1-64413-672-0

ebook ISBN 978-1-64413-673-7

Library of Congress Control Number: 2022942995

First printing

To Eleanor, vocalist and a Royal Academy voice in sacred music; Stephen, Marine Corps officer and gentleman; Anne Marie, exceptional teacher and coach; Joseph, officer from West Point and future lawyer; John, teacher and extraordinary coach; Michael Augustine, Coast Guardman and historian; and Mary Claire, artist and teacher. Because of these sons and daughters, I have experienced true happiness.

To St. Thomas Aquinas, who remarked:

> It is impossible for any created good to constitute man's happiness. For happiness is the perfect good, which lulls the appetite altogether; else it would not be the last end, if something yet remained to be desired. Now the object of the will, i.e. of man's appetite, is the universal good; just as the object of the intellect is the universal true. Hence it is evident that naught can lull man's will, save the universal good. This is to be found, not in any creature, but in God alone; because every creature has goodness by participation. (*Summa Theologica*, I–II, q. 2, art. 8 at Respondeo)

Contents

Preface xi

1. Aristotle and Aquinas: Backgrounds and Relevance to the Modern World 1

2. Defining Happiness 21

3. Happiness: Wealth, Money, and Material Possessions . . 47

4. Happiness: Fame, Power, and Honor 71

5. Is Happiness Derived from the Body and Pleasure? 97

6. Happiness: Family, Relationships, Marriage, and Children 143

7. Happiness, Spiritual Belief, and Religion 187

8. The Rules and Recipe for a Happy Life 221

About the Author 233

Figures and Tables

Figure 1. National Drug Overdose Deaths, Number among All Ages, 1999–2019 xiii

Figure 2. Percentage of Participants Endorsing Each Factor as a Consideration in Child Suicide Determination. xiv

Figure 1.1. Bust of Aristotle. Marble, Roman copy after a Greek bronze original by Lysippos from 330 BC; the alabaster mantle is a modern addition. Ludovisi Collection. *Source:* Photographer Giovanni Dall'Orto, March 2005 4

Figure 1.2. Excavation of the Lyceum. 6

Figure 1.3. Aristotle, Holding His *Ethics*. Raphael, 1510–1511 7

Figure 1.4. Saint Thomas Aquinas. Carlo Crivelli, 1476. 11

Figure 1.5. Apotheosis of St. Thomas Aquinas. Francisco de Zurbaran, 1631 13

Figure 1.6. Triumph of St. Thomas Aquinas over Averroes. Benozzo Gozzoli, 1471. 18

Table 2.1. Aristotle's Virtues and Vices .34

Figure 2.1. Increase in Opioid Overdoses since 1999 36

Figure 2.2. Opioid Statistics Are Mind-Numbing and Increasingly on the Rise 37

Figure 3.1. President Ronald Reagan Presents Mother Teresa with the Presidential Medal of Freedom at a White House Ceremony as First Lady Nancy Reagan Looks On, June 20, 1985 48

Figure 3.2. Effect of Annual Income on Happiness 50

Table 3.1. Population Growth Rates 61

Figure 3.3. Congresswoman Alexandria Ocasio-Cortez of New York, Advocate for Single-Payer Health System, the "Green New Deal," and Free College, Is Unabashedly a Democratic Socialist 64

Figure 3.4. Senator Bernie Sanders, Avowed Democratic Socialist. . . .68

Figure 4.1. Life Expectancy of Pop Musicians. Reprinted with permission of Dr. Dianna Theadora Kenney from her article "Stairway to Hell: Life and Death in the Pop Music Industry," as published in *The Conversation* 73

Figure 4.2. Charities Overpaying for Fundraisers. Reprinted with permission from Charity Navigator 82
Figure 4.3. The Honorable Speaker of the House, Nancy Pelosi 85
Figure 4.4. Last Picture of Adolf Hitler in the Crumbling Reichstag, April 28, 1945 86
Figure 4.5. Joseph Stalin: Ruler of the Soviet World 88
Figure 4.6. Department of Defense: U.S. Howitzer Attacks on ISIS Positions 90
Figure 4.7. Amy Winehouse Singing at the Virgin Festival, Pimlico, Baltimore, Maryland, on August 4, 2007 93
Figure 5.1. Relationship of Mind, Body, and Soul 99
Table 5.1. Love versus Lust 102
Figure 5.2. Sexual Activity Delay versus Happiness. *Source*: CDC, National Center for Health Statistics, National Survey of Family Growth, 1995 106
Figure 5.3. Potential Associations between Delayed Sexual Activity and Depression 107
Figure 5.4. Plastic Surgeon Expenditures 108
Figure 5.5. Reported STDs in the United States Reach All-Time High for Sixth Consecutive Year. More than 2.5 Million Cases of Chlamydia, Gonorrhea, and Syphilis Were Reported in 2019 114
Figure 5.6. Delay in Sexual Activity Cuts the Odds of Contracting STDs 115
Table 5.2. Risk of STD by Gender 121
Figure 5.7. Drug Use Increase, 1970–2014 122
Figure 5.8. Women, Depression, and Sexual Activity 124
Table 5.3. Depression and Sexual Activity 126
Figure 5.9. Attempted Suicide and Sexual Activity in Teenage Girls . . 127
Figure 5.10. Attempted Suicide and Sexual Activity in Teenage Boys . 127
Figure 5.11. Find Easy-to-Understand Drug Facts at https://teens.drugabuse.gov/teens/drug-facts 132
Figure 5.12. Use of Drugs, Individuals Aged Twelve and Over 134
Figure 5.13. Tetrahydrocannabinol (THC) Impacts Marked in Yellow from Marijuana Use 135

Figure 5.14. Drug Use in Centre County, PA 137
Figure 5.15. Age Distribution of Drug-Related Overdoses in PA, 2015–2017 137
Figure 6.1. The Unabomber. Courtesy of the FBI 145
Figure 6.2. The Unabomber's Montana Home. Courtesy of the FBI 145
Figure 6.3. Post-traumatic Stress Disorder Is a Significant or Extreme Emotional or Psychological Response to a Shocking, Dangerous, or Traumatic Event. It Affects Approximately 7 percent of the U.S. Population and 12–18 percent of Combat Veterans Deployed to Iraq and Afghanistan. U.S. Air Force photo by Senior Airman Christian Clausen/Released 147
Figure 6.4. Marriage Rates: United States, 1900–2018. 158
Figure 6.5. Percent of U.S. Births out of Wedlock 159
Figure 6.6. Active Shooter Incident Statistics. 161
Figure 6.7. Teenage Depression Rates 166
Figure 6.8. Living Arrangements of Children under Eighteen, 1968–2020. 168
Figure 6.9. Fertility Rates 176
Figure 7.1. Relationship between Religion and Health Outcomes . . . 190
Figure 7.2. Religion and Well-Being 191
Figure 7.3. Sisters of Notre Dame 195
Figure 7.4. Lourdes, France, Where Many Seek Miraculous Intervention. Seventy Official Miracles Declared—One as Recent as a French Nun in February 2018 200
Figure 7.5. The Incorruptible Body of St. John Southworth in Westminster Cathedral, London 202
Figure 7.6. Essentials of Christian Identity, Part One 206
Figure 7.7. Essentials of Christian Identity, Part Two 207
Figure 7.8 Property Defaced and Minks Released at This Site in Protest. Courtesy of the FBI 209
Figure 7.9. Forming Consciences for Faithful Citizenship 213

Preface

The quest for human happiness is a universal hope and ambition. Everyone seeks happiness over other negative states of being; in fact, it is an inherent quality, a yearning natural to our human constitution. While some have argued that human beings are by nature inclined to all that is good in life, there are those who speak of the battle between good and evil that gives rise to inner turmoil and conflict, while others observe that our fallen nature, due to sin and corruption, makes happiness an elusive endgame. Whatever vision one might adopt, all would agree that our goal is to be happy rather than distressed or sad; to be content and peaceful with every aspect of life whether in family or community, love and friendship, marriage and commitment. Everyone everywhere prefers happiness to distress, joy to despondency, optimism to pessimism, and a positive outlook from a life well lived over depression that results from personal failure. Nothing stated here need be corroborated or empirically, scientifically proven. Simple human observation can reach these conclusions.

If happiness be so universally sought, why are so many people miserably unhappy? In contemporary culture, the evidence for unhappiness rages like torrents and wild waves in a tsunami in all corners of the globe. To be sure, COVID dynamics do not foster happiness in many circles of human activity. While it is convenient to blame COVID for rising drugs, crime, suicide, and addiction rates, a person who understands the real meaning of happiness will not accept—even during these challenging days—that COVID can really kill true happiness. If anything, a crisis should make us all the more aware of what the real meanings of happiness and joy are. But it is undeniable that people have sunk a bit over the last few years, that their outlooks have been altered to the negative. For this reason alone, the pursuit of true and meaningful happiness has never been more important.

The challenges to happiness are everywhere and in every corner of human operations. The opioid crisis manifests more than a mere addiction, but a craving for artificial happiness. See figure 1.[1]

Alcoholism and drug abuse have reached staggering levels where millions of American citizens labor under the addictive influence, almost all of it driven by a desire to be happy or to escape what may be too difficult to bear. The general population seeks out psychiatric and psychological help in escalating numbers, all pining for solutions to emotional and behavioral problems, all hoping for some solution to the many underpinnings of sadness and unhappiness.

Suicide rates prove directly how formidable this lack of happiness can be, with it particularly tough on the younger citizen, the

[1] CDC WONDER, "Overdose Death Rates," Centers for Disease Control and Prevention WONDER online database, released December 2020, at https://www.drugabuse.gov/drug-topics/trends-statistics/overdose-death-rates.

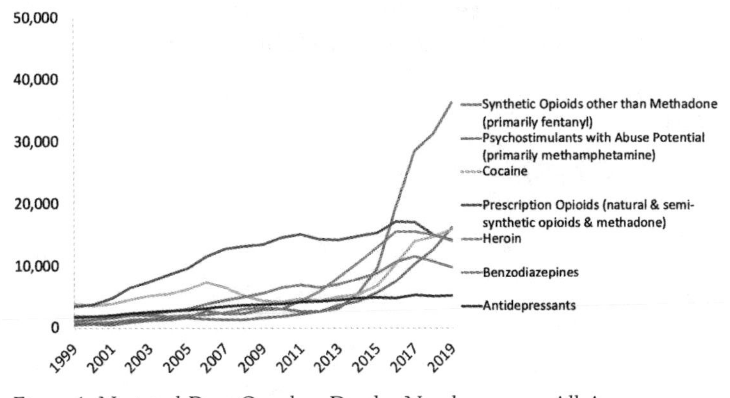

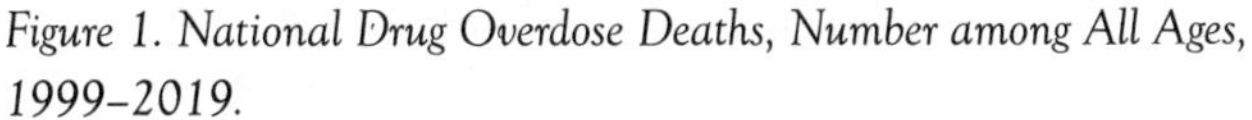

Figure 1. National Drug Overdose Deaths, Number among All Ages, 1999–2019.

high school or college student who ends life because that person can find no joy to continue or maintain existence. Even amongst children between the ages of ten and fourteen years, the rates of suicide continue their unabated trek upwards.[2] A recent empirical study of these pediatric suicide rates, based on the analysis of cause of death published by the medical examiners conducting autopsies, paints a frightening picture of children engaged in risky activity, already laden with child abuse histories or other psychological and psychiatric trauma. Remember, these are children between the ages of ten and fourteen, and the factors correlating to their suicides are charted at figure 2.[3]

[2] Franci Crepeau-Hobson, "The Psychological Autopsy and Determination of Child Suicides: A Survey of Medical Examiners," *Archives of Suicide Research* 14, no. 1 (2010): 24–34.

[3] Ibid. at table 1, 28.

Percentage of Participants Endorsing Each Factor as a Consideration in Child Suicide Determination

Factor	Percent
History of Suicidality	98.9
Suicide Note	100
Mood	86
Psychosocial stressors	92
Alcohol/Drug abuse history	61
Psychological history/Diagnosed mental disorders	97.8
Medical history	92
Death history of family	79
Educational/Employment history	79
History of child abuse	79
History of participating in choking games	85
Pre-suicidal behaviors	92
Sexual orientation	60

Figure 2. Percentage of Participants Endorsing Each Factor as a Consideration in Child Suicide Determination

Even more perplexing are the growing numbers of people committing suicide who lack any past history of mental disorder or psychiatric problems. While most research still finds a connection between suicide and psychological and psychiatric conditions, it appears a new and novel breed of suicide participant is impossibly emerging—a blank, emotionless actor lacking past mental disorders that explain the suicidal act.[4] Could it be that modern society is now fashioning or nurturing a new type of human agency that is utterly devoid of the usual and predictable emotional and intellectual qualities once predictive of suicide? Or, as a recent study once opined, that our conclusions about suicide might "reflect a bias in psychiatry towards classifying 'sadness' as an abnormal experience"?[5] One can only hope this trend never fully materializes. Other trends in suicide, especially among middle school, high school, and college-age students, can only distress, for despite a host of advantages never experienced in older generations, the discontent seems impenetrable. No matter how materially well cared for, no matter how advantaged in school and career paths, no matter how day-to-day needs are never for want, the question of suicide statistically rises. A study of Silicon Valley, California, students, raised in one of the wealthiest regions of the country, with incalculable advantages for a future life, manifests data demonstrating a "10-year suicide rate for the two high schools is between four and five times the national average."[6] The study tackles many controversial rationales for the enhanced suicide rates, but it speaks loudly on how material success, in and of itself, cannot foster an environment of self-worth, self-flourishing, and happiness.

4 Allison Milner, Jerneja Sveticic, and Diego De Leo, "Suicide in the Absence of Mental Disorder? A Review of Psychological Autopsy Studies across Countries," *International Journal of Social Psychiatry* 59, no. 6 (September 2013): 545–554.

5 Ibid., 552.

6 Hanna Rosin, "The Silicon Valley Suicides," *The Atlantic*, December 2015, 4, https://www.theatlantic.com/magazine/archive/2015/12/the-silicon-valley-suicides/413140/.

Similar results were discovered in an upscale Connecticut school, and when compared to poorer, far less advantaged schools, the results on suicide could not have been more similar. The results, conducted by Yale's psychiatry professor Suniya Luthar, concluded:

> At each extreme—poor and rich—kids are showing unusually high rates of dysfunction. On the surface, the rich kids seem to be thriving. They have cars, nice clothes, good grades, easy access to health care, and, on paper, excellent prospects. But many of them are not navigating adolescence successfully.
>
> The rich middle- and high-school kids Luthar and her collaborators have studied show higher rates of alcohol and drug abuse on average than poor kids, and much higher rates than the national norm. They report clinically significant depression or anxiety or delinquent behaviors at a rate two to three times the national average.[7]

In addition, addictive behaviors, whether in sex, gambling, or food and eating disorders, are rising at levels once unthinkable, for in each of these behaviors the void of unhappiness can be filled—at least artificially and very temporarily. Other forms of mania try, however ineffectively, to foster happiness, like unchecked material possessions and shopping sprees, dream homes and vacations, endless impulse buying and purging only to repeat the cycle again. All of these behaviors are imitators of happiness rather than the sum and substance of happiness. So too with the lust for fame and power: one will be happy if one becomes a famous actor or entertainer, a

[7] Ibid., 14. For the full study, see https://www.researchgate.net/publication/8964230_The_Culture_of_Affluence_Psychological_Costs_of_Material_Wealth.

politico with high title and authority, a personality whose face is plastered on every medium, especially on social media. However, all are bound to come up short in that journey to real happiness. So also will the desire for unlimited sex, to live a promiscuous life with partners left uncalculated in a hedonistic frenzy that satisfies merely one facet of the human person while neglecting so many others. The recent rash of porn actor deaths from suicide makes plain the darkness and emptiness of any world rooted in sexual pleasure alone. Then there are the obsessions over celebrity, that new class of artificial personality whose real contribution, aside from being a personality, is impossible to discover except for the invented celebrity and notoriety. None of this really brings meaningful happiness. Television, movies, and video games also are treated like distractions and stopgap measures in a world fraught with unhappiness. New religions and movements, new spiritual fads and cults try to pave over the holes as well. All around us, the world witnesses a population in deep distress as active shooters and killers roam our streets with extraordinary regularity.

The role of faith and belief, under traditional religious definitions, especially the Judeo-Christian ethic, has been swept away in favor of suspect theology. Church attendance rates continue their downward spiral—replaced with relative, stream-of-consciousness spiritualities like Cabala or Scientology, all of which are incapable of vanquishing or replacing the truth about God and creation. Marriage occurs far later in life when compared to historical realities, if in fact it occurs at all. The procreative function and propagation of human life has undergone a radical transformation by and through abortion, artificial birth control, abortifacients, the morning-after pill and the day-before pill. Children are born in smaller numbers as the nuclear family continues its slow trek to extinction. What children are born are either lavishly spoiled due to over-attention in the mold of parachute and helicopter parents, or severely neglected due to the parent's negligence, selfishness, or treatment of offspring as incidental nuisances.

At every juncture of human life and human operations, we encounter individuals and the community under moral, physical, and spiritual challenge. To soften this void, we engage every sort of "ism" as a substitute purpose for human life, whether it be *environmentalism*; *communism* and its penchant for economic redistribution; *materialism* as its own good; *atheism* and *agnosticism*, where nothing can be demonstrated and thus cannot be believed; *egoism*, that narrow and exclusive pursuit of self-interest as one's only aim or purpose; *nihilism*, which purports that nothing in reality is provable; or moral *relativism*, which denies absolute, universal, and perennial ethical principles in favor of a transient, almost whimsical moral order. Each of these schools of thought falter and foster a personal and communal unease, and even desolation, all at the expense of happiness.

Our politicians, our Church leaders, our entertainers and sports stars have let us down in immeasurable ways. Congress and other governmental authorities have even lower popularity than hardened criminals. No one has much faith in once vaunted and respected institutions, whether it be the Catholic Church's handling of the sexual abuse crisis or the self-enrichment tactics of congresspersons and senators. None of these conditions lead to human happiness, yet this is precisely the current merry-go-round the world provides. At a whirling pace, the inhabitants of this planet encounter these forces and movements, so briskly and speedily that the human agent cannot properly adjudge most of it. Modern life has become so tumultuous and inexact that it is no wonder there are so many who are depressed, so many who end life prematurely, so many who need intervention to cope, and so, so many who must prop themselves up using artificial mechanisms to be "happy."

For high school and college students the problems are becoming more than acute, and more so as the COVID crisis labors on. After a lifetime working with young people, from middle school and high school students to undergraduate and graduate students, and even at the doctoral level, I have gazed upon this steady and inevitable decline in my students' well-being since 1977. I have no faith in any current or modern fad that holds itself as a remedy for unhappiness. In fact, I have never been more convinced that real, meaningful happiness should not depend upon the modern potions bandied about for personal contentment. Indeed, these attractive alternatives work for but a moment in time, and the remedy needed has to be of stronger and longer-term mettle. I have also researched, studied, and applied these fundamental questions in a host of writings and lectures and keep finding myself coming back to two of the West's greatest thinkers, namely Aristotle and Thomas Aquinas—both of whom have elaborate and highly developed examinations of the concept of happiness. I am firmly and resolutely convinced of their current relevancy because both thinkers offer up an unrivaled blueprint for human fulfillment—a plan worthy of our admiration.

Both thinkers studied and systematized happiness in ways that have contemporary meaning. Aristotle's masterpiece, the *Nicomachean Ethics*, a work so significant that Aquinas wrote a massive commentary on its wisdom and applicability fifteen hundred years after its authorship, delivers a recipe for human life and human happiness. The *Ethics* lays out the processes that lead to human productivity and flourishing—key elements on the road to happiness. Aristotle's examination of happiness, which he terms *eudaimonia*, is totally complemented by Aquinas's *Treatise on Happiness*—a part of his massive *Summa Theologica*. In Aristotle, we encounter a pagan believing in many gods, while in Aquinas, the Angelic Doctor and most formidable intellect in the history of Christianity, a Catholic representing the dogma and doctrines of his Faith with accuracy and intellectual brilliance. Both seriously address the question of human happiness and contentment.

Hence, this short text is a "Recipe for Life," or "Rules for a Happy Life," fully grounded and dependent upon Aristotle and Aquinas. It is a mix and formula for human happiness that may be meaningful to those in search of a more tranquil state. Unfolding on the pages to come will be a reliable path to human contentment, personal fulfillment, and happiness—not a perfect, exhilarating happiness without interruption or pause. Instead, this recipe and these rules deliver the type of peace and tranquility only possible with a clear understanding of the world around us, the place we fit into the overall scheme of things, and the day-to-day steps and questions needed to be taken and posed to achieve a happy life. For Aristotle and Aquinas will pose clear and cutting questions in this search for human contentment, including but not limited to:

- Will virtue lead to happiness?
- Will wealth and material possessions lead to happiness?
- Will fame, glory, honor, and power lead to happiness?
- Will pleasure, sensuality, and sexuality lead to happiness?
- Will marriage and family life lead to happiness?
- Will religion and the spiritual life lead to happiness?

From these and many other questions, the reader will discover a pathway, a road and river that can and does lead to a life filled with human happiness—a world very, very different than the purposeless whirlwind described above.

1

Aristotle and Aquinas: Backgrounds and Relevance to the Modern World

Introduction

Few thinkers have had as much impact on the intellectual, moral, and philosophical history of the West as Aristotle and Thomas Aquinas. Aside from their prolific capacities to write, to lecture, and to dissect and examine problems in ways scholars simply marvel at, each provides foundational insights into the goodness or evil of human activity. Each grapples with ethical dilemmas; the distinction between virtue and vice; and the nature, purpose, and ultimate end for human existence. From studies of the heavens to biological function, from politics to law and justice, from the temporal to the transcendent, both thinkers make major contributions. And despite being sixteen centuries apart, these two thinkers are not only conceptually compatible in most respects but also intellectually entangled in very intimate ways. For Thomas Aquinas, the Angelic Doctor of Roman Catholicism, was a great, almost passionate admirer of Aristotle, referring to him as "the Philosopher" without match or equivalent that he had encountered. This conclusion alone is remarkable given Thomas's thirteenth-century reality where most philosophical and theological studies were highly restricted in the confines of Church positions.

Just as Aristotle broke with Plato's theory of the forms, where a secondary perfect reality of things existed to a reality-based philosophy, an idea quite radical for his time, so too Thomas, whose intellectual affection for the Greeks and the Romans, in the mold of Plato and Aristotle, Cicero and Seneca, was equally radical. Each thinker displays a mind on fire with ideas and intellectual rigor, and each seems to complement the other. While there is dispute in this quarter, many conclude that Thomas "harmonizes" Aristotle's pagan conclusions about a well-lived and happy life using natural reason with Thomas's equal agreement coupled with Christian revelation.[8] Others describe the compatibility between the two as Thomas's successful Christianization of Aristotle, for only then does the philosophical system of Aristotle reach its ultimate and perfect conclusion. What is all the more striking about these two figures, especially when backgrounds are considered, is how close in thought and conclusions, although admittedly un-identical, these philosophical giants are. Aristotle, a passionate advocate of natural reason and its capacity to discover truth, meets up with Aquinas, who fully agrees with the power of reason and then expands those positions into the revealed and salvific world of Christianity. It may sound trite, but for the most part, each gets to the same destination.

For the purposes of this examination, that of happiness, Aristotle and Aquinas travel side by side despite theological differences. In matters of ethics, virtue, the end and good we seek, and, most importantly, the road to and achievement of happiness, it would

[8] Harry Jaffa, *Thomism and Aristotelianism* (Chicago: University of Chicago Press, 1952), 22.

be difficult to find more compatible thinkers. For as Harry Jaffa points out in his piercing work, *Thomism and Aristotelianism*, they both reach similar conclusions on those issues central to the question of human happiness, namely:

1. Belief in divine particular providence
2. Belief that perfect happiness is impossible in this life
3. Belief in the necessity of personal immortality to complete the happiness intended, evidently, by nature
4. Belief in personal immortality
5. Belief in the special creation of individual souls
6. Belief in a divinely implanted "natural" habit of the moral principles[9]

These mutual conclusions are more than significant in the matter of happiness, for Aristotle and Aquinas write for neither the pagan nor the Christian alone but for the whole of humanity. Their observations lay out a "recipe" for human existence no matter what group, ethnicity, religion or creed, nationalized status or citizenship. To do otherwise would be a disastrous formula for the select few. Aristotle and Aquinas write of happiness in universal tones with worldwide applicability, not by sect or city. Their suggestions for a happy existence are also quite timeless, for what is true for Aristotle in 365 BC was just as true for Thomas in the mid-thirteenth century. For the reader, be assured that these timeless suggestions on happiness have yet to be shown flawed or faulty. None of these recommendations for a happy life go out of favor or change by a fluid relativity and instead remain constant, permanent, and universal criteria on how to achieve a happy existence.

[9] Ibid., 187.

Figure 1.1. Bust of Aristotle. Marble, Roman copy after a Greek bronze original by Lysippos from 330 BC; the alabaster mantle is a modern addition. Ludovisi Collection. Source: Photographer Giovanni Dall'Orto, March 2005.

Aristotle (384–322 BC)

Aristotle, the greatest and most productive of all Greek philosophers (see figure 1.1[10]), was born in 384 BC.[11]

His father, Nicomachus, a court physician to the king of Macedon, King Amyntus III, died while Aristotle was still a young boy. Aristotle was sent to Athens at age seventeen by his guardian to

[10] Ancient portrait of Aristotle, mounted on a semiprecious stone bust, preserved in the Altemps Palace, Rome. Ludovisi Collection photo by Giovanni Dall'Orto, March 2005.

[11] P. M. Dunn, "Aristotle (384–322 BC): Philosopher and Scientist of Ancient Greece," *Archives of Disease in Childhood: Fetal and Neonatal Edition* 91, no. 1 (January 2006): F75–F77.

pursue an unrivaled education for his time.[12] For a total of twenty years, Aristotle studied under the eye and guidance of Plato in his academy and eventually became a teacher.[13] Plato recognized Aristotle's gifted academic qualities, though each, while agreement was continuous and constant, did differ on some essential philosophical principles.[14] Plato suggests that the *form* of created things, what the thing is made of, is separate from the thing that one senses or sees. In short, Plato's world consisted of a perfect template for anything, such as a bed or chair, tree or plant, and what we encounter in the real world a copy or image of that. Aristotle strenuously moved into a more realistic philosophical position, arguing that the essence or form is in the thing itself.[15]

Plato died in 347 BC, but Aristotle was not appointed to succeed him in the governance of the Academy.[16] It was a result of his differences with Plato, but nevertheless Aristotle lived in Asia Minor, pursuing his studies in biology and natural history.[17] In 342 BC, he was called to Macedon by King Phillip II to tutor his son Alexander, who would become Alexander the Great. While Alexander set out to conquer the Persian Empire, Aristotle, aged forty-nine, returned to Athens and established his own school of philosophy, the Lyceum.[18] See figure 1.2.[19]

[12] Ibid.
[13] Ibid.
[14] Ibid.
[15] J. Sachs, "Aristotle: Metaphysics," *Internet Encyclopedia of Philosophy*, accessed May 25, 2019, https://www.iep.utm.edu/aris-met.
[16] Dunn, "Aristotle," F75–F77.
[17] Ibid.
[18] Ibid.
[19] Photo by Mirjanamimi, Wikimedia Commons user, accessed March 1, 2019, https://commons.wikimedia.org/wiki/File:Aristotle_Lyceum.jpg. This file is licensed under the Creative Commons

Figure 1.2. Excavation of the Lyceum.

At this school Aristotle lectured, wrote a large majority of his philosophical treatises and dialogues, and collected books, in effect creating the first library in European history.[20] Aristotle was nicknamed "Peripatetic" after *peripatos*, stretches of main road where he had the habit of lecturing as he walked along the way.[21] In 323 BC, when news of Alexander's death in Babylon reached Athens, Aristotle left Athens and moved to Chalcis in Euboea, his mother's hometown. It was there that he died of a stomach illness the following year.[22]

Attribution-ShareAlike 4.0 International license, https://creativecommons.org/licenses/by-sa/4.0/.

20 W. Morrison, "The Lyceum," *Internet Encyclopedia of Philosophy*, accessed May 25, 2019, https://www.iep.utm.edu/lyceum.

21 Dunn, "Aristotle," F75–F77.

22 Ibid.

Figure 1.3. Aristotle, Holding His Ethics. *Raphael, 1510–1511.*

After his death, Aristotle's pupils kept all his writings in a vault, for fear of theft.[23] The dampness of the vault somewhat damaged the writings, which were discovered about two hundred years after the death of Aristotle. In 86 BC the writings moved from Athens to Rome, where they attracted a great many scholars, and a new edition of them gave a new rise to the study of Aristotle and of philosophy.[24] Over the decades of his career as a teacher, Aristotle's lectures amassed to nearly 150 volumes. This vast number of volumes soon represented an encyclopedia of the knowledge of his time, and most of the contribution was of his own work.[25] Though he is known as one of the greatest philosophers in the world, Aristotle also worked with biology, psychology, politics, poetry, drama, and ethics.[26] Most, if not all, of the areas of knowledge Aristotle investigated he went on to transform with his studies, observations, and writings.[27] See figure 1.3.[28]

23 "Aristotle (384–322 BCE)," *Internet Encyclopedia of Philosophy*, accessed May 25, 2019, https://www.iep.utm.edu/aristotl.

24 Ibid.

25 Dunn, "Aristotle," F75–F77.

26 Ibid.

27 "Aristotle (384–322 BCE)," *Internet Encyclopedia*.

28 Aristotle, holding his *Ethics*, Raphael, 1510–1511.

Aristotle developed a formal system for reasoning, which earned him the title "father of the field of logic."[29] Aristotle's writings on logic were grouped under the name *Organon*, or instrument, derived from the perspective that logic and reasoning were "the chief preparatory instrument of scientific investigation."[30]

Aristotle's great work *Metaphysics* raised questions that dealt with things that make us human, from the definition of *ousia*, or being, to what constitutes matter and form. Aristotle begins *Metaphysics* with a sketch of the history of philosophy, which he believes grew from the feeling of curiosity of the world. The logical inquiries of *Metaphysics* stem from its central questions of being, things, and what makes things "things."[31] For Aristotle, metaphysics "deals with the first principles of scientific knowledge and the ultimate conditions of all existence."[32] Aristotle observed the world and wondered at its movements. From his observations he realized that everything in the world, from rocks to plants to humans, is always busy as it continues to be itself, to advance or preserve itself—something that is not necessarily a theory as much as it is the reality of the world.[33]

In *Metaphysics*, Aristotle introduces the idea of form and matter. Matter is the underlying structure of changes, in which there is something constant as things change in growth or decay; it is the potential of something, the capacity to change; it is contingent and without specific qualities; once it is actualized (all the potentials of the thing are realized), then it is identical with form.[34] The development of potentiality to actuality was intended

[29] "Aristotle (384–322 BCE)," *Internet Encyclopedia.*

[30] Ibid.

[31] Sachs, "Metaphysics."

[32] "Aristotle (384–322 BCE)," *Internet Encyclopedia.*

[33] Ibid.

[34] Ibid.

to help the earlier thinkers with their questions of existence and its beginnings.[35]

Though known for his philosophical work, Aristotle made great contributions to the fields of botany, zoology, anatomy, embryology, and physiology.[36] His great observation of nature that lent him knowledge found in *Metaphysics* also assisted him in the knowledge of the human body. Unable to study the internal structure of the human body, Aristotle studied animals, dissecting over fifty different species, thus founding the science of comparative anatomy.[37]

His most significant contributions in philosophy, however, relate to his virtue theory and his analysis of proper ends and goods for the human person. His masterpiece, the *Nicomachean Ethics*, is still considered by many to be the seminal work on virtue theory, as well as a plan for a well-lived life. Of particular interest to this examination of happiness is how proper judgments about human conduct are best derived from reason rather than the will and how reason instructs or guides us on the proper courses of conduct in human life. In addition, his ethical works keenly and precisely examine a series of virtues and vices and comparatively lay out the results of choosing either. In fact, the most significant insight posed on virtue theory is that it discerns the "mean" of human activity as the norm—nothing in excess or deficit in most cases. By *mean* we do not imply a simple middle or compromise position in human activity—a sort of middle ground where some conduct in every form is acceptable as long as it is not excessive or, in some special cases, undertaken at all. The mean is the balance sought for virtuous action, and in some cases the mean requires a rejection of any participation, as in immoral and

35 Ibid.

36 Dunn, "Aristotle," F75–F77.

37 Ibid.

universally condemned activity such as incest, bestiality, pedophilia, and murder. In these cases, a life of moderation is an impossibility—a life of avoidance the only acceptable measure and mean. But in most other behaviors, there is something to be said about the maxim, derivable from Aristotle, that *everything should be in moderation*—not in excess or complete deficit. So, to be just, one gives another what is due, not less or more. In courage, one may be fearless but not so exaggerated that a life suffers loss without due introspection, or in temperance when we measure slavishness to food or drink or other things rather than enjoy in moderation. Hence, Aristotle delivers a context of measurement in human action, often seeking the mean of this act or that conduct, so that ethical and moral action can be identified. This testing of things is part and parcel of his happiness formula. Part of the reason Aristotle has such a cohesive theory of happiness is because he is willing to tackle human conduct at base and particular levels. So enthralled is Aquinas with the *Nicomachean Ethics* that he wrote a massive text and commentary on it.[38]

"The Philosopher's" works became a central underpinning of all philosophical pursuits even to the present day, influencing Roman and Byzantine Christian philosophy in the West and Arabic philosophy in the East. Indeed, the glory of the Islamic world during the time of Avicenna and Averroes can be directly tied to its desire for and wholehearted adoption of Aristotelianism. Some have argued that a return to this school would be very beneficial when compared to the current strife in the Muslim world.

In the contemporary philosophical world, the power and persuasiveness of Aristotle's thought continue to dominate the debate and didactic about what is good, what is just, what is the ultimate

[38] St. Thomas Aquinas, *Commentary on Aristotle's Nicomachean Ethics*, trans. C. J. Litzinger (Notre Dame, IN: Dumb Ox Books, 1993).

Figure 1.4. Saint Thomas Aquinas. Carlo Crivelli, 1476.

end we seek as human beings. And in the end, this approach is the best path to human happiness.

St. Thomas Aquinas (1225–1274)

A life as rich and as productive as that of Aquinas (figure 1.4) is difficult to summarize in a few pages.

The life and times of Thomas Aquinas have been the subject of some exceptional biographies and other studies that highlight the enormity of his influence.[39] That he is a Doctor of the Church, a

[39] Some representative biographies and critiques include but are not limited to James Weisheipl, *Friar Thomas D'Aquino: His Life, Thought, and Work*, 1st ed. (Garden City, NY: Doubleday, 1974);

patron of Catholic education, and designated the Angelic Doctor of Roman Catholicism[40] is testimony to both his spiritual depth and breadth and his immense intellect. On the flip side of these designations are a series of caricatures that follow Thomas wherever his thought is considered—Thomas the churchman, the papist, the theologian, and the dogmatic enforcer. Anyone who seriously encounters the body of work produced by St. Thomas can discern the folly of these descriptors, for in Aquinas one witnesses a colossal philosophical genius.

St. Thomas was clearly not from humble beginnings. The Italian family of Aquino was linked to Lombard kings and several royal houses of Europe. Landulph, his father, held the titles of Count of Aquino and Lord of Loreto, Acerro, and Belcastro. As nephew of Emperor Frederick Barbarossa, he was also connected to the family of King Louis IX of France. His wife, Theodora, was the Countess of Teano, a part of Sicily conquered by Norman barons.[41] St. Thomas, born in Roccasecca around 1225, comes from a distinguished family with the usual high expectations for its offspring. From an early age, St. Thomas displayed an uncanny intellectual ability and as a result was sent to exceptional schools with high expectations for a significant career in military, political, or clerical service. After a classical education

---

Frederick Copleston, *Aquinas: An Introduction to the Life and Work of the Great Medieval Thinker* (New York: Penguin Books, 1991); Ralph M. McInerny, *St. Thomas Aquinas* (Notre Dame, IN: University of Notre Dame Press, 1982).

[40] Pope Benedict XV, encyclical letter *Fausto appetente die* (June 29, 1921), AAS 13, 332; Pope Pius XI, encyclical letter *Studiorum ducem* (June 29, 1923), AAS 15, §11.

[41] See Joseph Vann, *Lives of Saints* (New York: John J. Crawley & Co., 1954).

Figure 1.5. Apotheosis of St. Thomas Aquinas. Francisco de Zurbaran, 1631.

at Monte Cassino and subsequent enrollment at the university in Naples, St. Thomas surprised his family with his decision to join the Dominicans—a new order founded by St. Dominic. So distraught was his family about this choice that his mother asked her other sons to confine Thomas at the castle at Monte San Giovanni Campano until his mind changed back to Monte Cassino. For more than a year, St. Thomas was kept within the castle walls,[42] although the family was unsuccessful in its efforts to change his decision.

His placement at the University of Paris in 1245 commenced an intellectual journey few have rivaled in the history of civilization. As a student, Thomas was exposed to his mentor, Albert the Great, whose influence and encouragement appeared unwavering from

[42] G.K. Chesterton, *St. Thomas Aquinas: The Dumb Ox* (Teddington, UK: Echo Library, 2007).

the outset.[43] While Albert witnessed an intellect with exceptional possibilities, most who had earlier encountered Thomas found him both quiet and unreservedly large and tall for his time. His student colleagues had labeled him the Dumb Ox, to which Albert retorted, "You call him the dumb ox, but in his teaching he will one day produce such a bellowing that it will be heard throughout the world."[44]

During his tenure at Paris, he worked closely with Albert and followed him on his subsequent appointment at Cologne. In his early professorial career, Thomas concentrated on Sacred Scripture and biblical studies and authored nearly fifty original pieces of scholarly text on the Old and New Testaments (see figure 1.5[45]).

At the same time, St. Thomas delved into all manner of theological and philosophical subject matter, working for decades to finish a massive compendium and theological and philosophical treatises. His first major synthesis on Peter Lombard's *Sentences* took three years to finish and delivered some early insights into Thomas's great penchant for ethical and jurisprudential insights. Vernon Bourke relays,

> In his early thirties, Thomas Aquinas was already well known as a brilliant scholar and teacher. His preparatory studies had been more thorough than those of most of his colleagues. He had read widely and profoundly in the available literature of contemporary science, philosophy and religion. He had studies at four great and dissimilar centers of learning: Monte Cassino, the state University

[43] Ibid.

[44] Eleanor Stump, *Aquinas* (Boston: Routledge Press, 2003), 3.

[45] *Apotheosis of St. Thomas Aquinas*, Francisco de Zurbaran, 1631.

of Naples, the Dominican Institute at Cologne and the University of Paris.[46]

His two other tomes, *Summa Contra Gentiles* and *Summa Theologica*, compiled between 1261 and 1267, encompass the fullness and comprehensiveness of Catholic philosophical and theological thought. Other works, commonly labeled *Academic Disputations*, were produced at lightning speed during the remainder of his academic life at Paris, Cologne, and Naples. His myriad of works covered topics including but not limited to truth, the power of God, the soul, evil, virtue, law, being and essence, and kingship.

It is simply impossible to give proper treatment to the vastness of Thomas's bibliography, the scope of which "belong to many fields of activity and are a faithful mirror of his participation in the religious and intellectual life of his age."[47] Anthony Kenny correctly types Thomas as an intellect "of extraordinary power and industry."[48] From immortality of the soul to kingship and tyranny, from good and evil, the full range of scholarly products cannot be readily catalogued, for even world political figures and high-ranking Church personnel solicited the opinions offered by Thomas.[49]

By 1252, his tutelage under Albert the Great ended, and he subsequently returned to the University of Paris for further study,

[46] Vernon J. Bourke, *The Pocket Aquinas: Selections from the Writings of St. Thomas* (New York: Washington Square Press, 1960), xv–xvi.

[47] Anton C. Pegis, *An Introduction to St. Thomas* (New York: The Modern Library, 1948), xii.

[48] Anthony Kenny, *Aquinas* (London: Oxford University Press, 1980), 19.

[49] I.T. Eschmann, O.P., "A Catalogue of St. Thomas' Works: Bibliographical Notes," in Etienne Gilson, *The Christian Philosophy of Saint Thomas Aquinas* (New York: Random House, 1956), 381–439.

culminating in the receipt of his license to teach theology at Paris in 1256. In 1259, Thomas was assigned to various teaching assignments in Italy at the papal Curia as well as Orvieto, Rome, and Viterbo from 1261 to 1268. At this time, Thomas expended a great deal of intellectual effort commenting and critiquing the works of "the Philosopher" Aristotle with special and incisive analysis on his ethical and virtue theory.[50] Couple his conceptual affection for Aristotle with his respect shown to Arabian thinkers like Avicenna and Averroes, as well as Jewish philosopher Maimonides, and what emerges is a theologian/philosopher without match. This is a mind that can be best described as boundless, vivified, and in constant yearning, living in what Pegis calls the "historically social character of his own philosophical work. He lives and thinks in the company of others."[51]

For example, Thomas's efforts to "assimilate Aristotelianism," the body of philosophical works of Aristotle, displayed his tendency to be intellectually open to every tradition that aided in the understanding of Catholic thought. At the time, studying pagans like Aristotle, Cicero, and Plato was frowned upon.[52] To be sure, St. Thomas was not a shrinking violet but a diorama of flowers bursting with colors ready to tackle reality at every level in which it could be comprehended.

To his more traditional colleagues, St. Thomas was operating at the fringes by his very generosity of mind and thought. In his last term at the University of Paris, his productivity reached its apex, culminating in the authorship of the second part of his *Summa Theologica*—over a million words in length—alongside the other texts he

[50] Aquinas, *Commentary*.

[51] Pegis, *Introduction to St. Thomas*, xiv.

[52] Bourke, *Pocket Aquinas*, xvii.

was simultaneously authoring. The sheer volume of his opus staggers even the modern observer. As Anthony Kenny remarks, "When one reviews the sheer bulk of his output between 1269–1273 one can believe the testimony of his chief secretary that it was his habit, like a grand master at a chess tournament, to dictate to three or four secretaries simultaneously; one can almost believe the further testimony that he could dictate coherent prose while he slept."[53]

After his second stint at the University of Paris, Thomas was asked by his Dominican superiors to create a Dominican house of study in Naples. During his travels to do so, he experienced a series of changes internally and externally that forever altered his once entrenched habits. Some have claimed that Thomas was mystically touched and was capable of levitation. He exhibited signs of mysterious inner prayer and religious fervor.[54] In one of his travels, while riding in an open cart, his head was struck by a low-hanging tree limb. In 1274, while recuperating at a monastery, his health continued its downward trend. After another mystical experience, Thomas indicated to his colleagues that his enormous body of work, when compared in the context of true divine knowledge, "seems like straw."[55] On his deathbed, St. Thomas Aquinas's last words to the Cistercian monks signify his peaceful acceptance of his impending demise: "This is my rest for ever and ever: here will I dwell, for I have chosen it" (Ps. 131:14).

Often called "the Universal Teacher," St. Thomas Aquinas died at the monastery of Fossanova on March 7, 1274.[56] He was

[53] Kenny, *Aquinas*, 25.

[54] Ibid., 26.

[55] Brian Davies, *The Thought of Thomas Aquinas* (Oxford: Oxford University Press, 1993), 9.

[56] Raïssa Maritain, *St. Thomas Aquinas: Angel of the Schools* (New York: Longmans, Green and Co., 1942), 108.

Figure 1.6. Triumph of St. Thomas Aquinas over Averroes. Benozzo Gozzoli, 1471.

canonized by Pope John XXII in 1323 and declared an Angelic Doctor by Pope Pius V in 1567.[57] In 1879, Pope Leo XIII characterized Thomas's theology as the definitive exposition of Catholic doctrine and decreed that all Catholic seminaries and universities be grounded in Thomism (see figure 1.6).[58]

In 1880, St. Thomas was declared patron of all Catholic educational institutions. The influence of Thomism has been subject to the ebb and flow of philosophical schools, none more compellingly antagonistic than those promoting ethical and moral relativity. In Thomas, the reader is exposed to a dependable system worthy of any intellectual: open yet resistant to chaos, fixed when it need be and subject to fine-tuning if justified. St. Thomas provides a methodology of truth, one "profoundly religious, sensitive to

[57] Leonardas V. Gerulaitis, "The Canonization of Saint Thomas Aquinas," *Vivarium* 5, no. 1 (1967): 25–46; *The Catholic Encyclopedia*, vol. 14 (New York: Robert Appleton Company, 1912), s.v. "St. Thomas Aquinas," by Daniel Kennedy, accessed March 16, 2015, http://www.newadvent.org/cathen/14663b.htm.

[58] *Triumph of St. Thomas Aquinas*, Benozzo Gozzoli, 1471.

the value of tradition," while "nonetheless an innovator in both philosophy and theology."[59] Anton Pegis labels Aquinas a "Giant":

> He stood on a giant past; and although he himself was a giant, he always looked upon his intellectual stature with the genuine humility of one who, even in his highest speculative reaches, accepted the fruits of philosophical victory as much as those who went before him as in his own.[60]

Rules for a Happy Life

1.0: Aristotle: Happiness Is an Activity of the Soul in Accordance with Complete Virtue.

1.1: Aquinas: God Is Happiness by His Essence: for He Is Happy not by Acquisition or Participation of Something Else but by His Essence.

[59] Bourke, *Pocket Aquinas*, xix.

[60] Pegis, *Introduction to St. Thomas*, xxx.

2

Defining Happiness

Aristotle

Happiness is living well and acting well.[61]

Happiness is self-sufficiency and the end of all human action.[62]

Aquinas

Happiness is the ultimate end of the human person.[63]

Happiness seeks the perfect good and the ultimate good which is God.[64]

Any formula for a happy life and internal happiness must start at the very beginning—discerning the goal of happiness by defining it as a state of being. The most profound question—"what is

61 Aristotle, *Nicomachean Ethics* [hereafter cited as *Nic. Ethics*], 1095a17–20.

62 *Nic. Ethics*, 1097b6–16.

63 St. Thomas Aquinas, *Treatise on Happiness*, 1.1.7.corp.

64 Ibid., 1.4–5.

happiness?"—must be tackled before issuing any advice on how one gets to the station in life where one truly is happy. The ancient Greeks tagged happiness as *eudaimonia*, a state signifying the "best kind of human life possible ... the summum bonum of a happy life."[65] *Eudaimonia* represents the many slivers and slants of what constitutes happiness including, but not limited to, a "mood" and a "life" or "flourishing" or "well-being."[66]

At every corner of the definition reside subjective opinions on what it means to be happy, yet at the same time those corners also edify objective measures that correlate to the idea of happiness—things like a rewarding professional and vocational life, friendships and family, health and emotional well-being, as well as a host of other variables that make for the happy person. Precisely how happiness is measured generally falls into two camps: first, those that claim it is a mental judgment about one's state of life and the general satisfaction that surrounds a life well lived, and second, a school that believes that happiness is merely affective, emotional, and/or a feeling that may or may not require judgment.[67] In a philosophical sense, the former school surely is the dominant one, holding that happiness is a mental state or a rational conclusion about the world and the life unfolding. Some hold that the happy person possesses a "happy temperament, a person who is inclined to feel happy or be in a good mood often."[68] While this definition has merit, it seems to be too subjective to pin down in any sense, for this view attempts to measure the

[65] Paul Bloomfield, "Morality Is Necessary for Human Life," *Philosophical Studies* 174, no. 10 (2017): 2618.

[66] Ibid., 2618.

[67] Alan H. Goldman, "Happiness Is an Emotion," *Journal of Ethics* 21, no. 1 (2017): 2–3.

[68] Ibid., 7.

immeasurable. On the other hand, making a judgment about one's current station in life—one's own sense of accomplishment or self-value—ties itself to performance objectives such as family life, an education, a willingness to use all abilities, and other factors. To be sure, there are no precise and universal definitions of what happiness connotes and encompasses. However, it is fair to say that some people are happier than others because of certain attributes and characteristics in a life well lived or organized. That is part of our pursuit in this guide and recipe for the happy human life—to identify those conditions that seem to foster happiness more readily and avoid those circumstances and events that produce an unhappy person.

Parameters and Limitations on Happiness

Of first consideration is whether happiness has parameters or limitations, at least in our day-to-day human existence and activity. Understanding happiness and the happy life is to know its boundaries. Most sensible people already know that a pristine and eternal state of happiness cannot be encountered in the temporal world. We know this because we, as human actors, are not always happy, happier, or happiest in every dimension of our daily life. Human life may wish for and hope for happiness all day, all night, and all the time, although this ambition is utterly and almost ridiculously impossible. To be happy all the time defeats the very notion of what happiness entails. No human life can pine for a perpetual form of happiness, at least in this temporal orb. Such craving might make perfect sense for the afterlife, the state of being after death if the rewards of Heaven are to be believed. In fact, both Aristotle and Aquinas were quite adamant that our imperfect constitution, moving through human existence as temporal actors, would never achieve that state of contentment in the here and now. That type of perpetual happiness is reserved for another dimension.

Aristotle

If anything is the gift of the gods to men it is reasonable to think that happiness, the best by far of all human actions, is the gift of God.[69]

Aquinas

Some participation in happiness can be had in this life, but true and perfect happiness cannot be had in this life. Now what is good in the present life is transitory, for life itself, which we naturally desire, passes away.[70]

So, in this sense, to understand happiness is to appreciate and approve its natural limitations in our day-to-day life. A clear problem in modern life has been this inordinate craving for constant, continuous, and uninterrupted happiness. Dr. Victor Frankl, a therapist who survived the Holocaust during World War II, captures this unrealistic yearning when he notes, "It is the very pursuit of happiness that thwarts happiness."[71]

[69] *Nic. Ethics*, 1099b11–14.

[70] Aquinas, *Happiness*, 1.5.3.corp.

[71] Viktor E. Frankl, *Man's Search for Meaning* (Boston: Beacon Press, 2006); Emily Esfahani Smith, "There's More to Life Than Being Happy," *The Atlantic*, January 9, 2013, https://www.theatlantic.com/health/archive/2013/01/theres-more-to-life-than-being-happy/266805/.

Hence, from the very outset it is crucial to understand the limitations of human happiness, for it cannot be constant, untouched, or unmoved, nor can it be a perpetual feeling or state of being. Instead, happiness modulates, increases, decreases, and even disappears in human activity. At no juncture in this Paradise Lost will happiness stick without fail but instead will be subject to an extraordinary range of levels and modifications. "While happiness is an emotion felt in the here and now, it ultimately fades away, just as all emotions do; positive affect and feelings of pleasure are fleeting. The amount of time people report feeling good or bad correlates with happiness but not at all with meaning."[72]

Happiness as Boundless Exhilaration or Contentment

Second, happiness should never be equated with an unrestricted or unbridled type of emotional exhilaration, a sort of overflowing emotional high that can never be fully maintained or sustained. Too often those seeking happiness will conceive of this state of being as frenetically, almost effervescently joyful, without moderation. Many believe that only when at this level has true happiness been achieved, but alas, such thinking contradicts the very essence of what happiness entails. Happiness constitutes many levels and types of experiences that vary from simple contentment to a peaceful, tranquil emotional equilibrium to a sense of well-being where everything and everyone around you makes sense and is in its proper place. Happiness may be properly defined as a generally stress-free environment or a confident personal outlook unhindered by fear and trepidation, or it might be suitably characterized as Dr. Robert Holden relays:

[72] Smith, "Happy."

> Happiness is life's most cherished goal. On every continent, in every country and in every culture, when people are asked, "What do you want?" the most popular answer is "happiness." When parents are asked, "What do you most want for your children?" the answer is "happiness." Happiness is the goal that makes other life goals—like success, prosperity and relationships—feel meaningful and enjoyable.[73]

Not a bad insight from an entertainer. Indeed, entertainers, by and large, may be in one of the worst occupations to keep happiness in its proper confines since they so often evaluate happiness in light of many extremes or deficits. They are often tossed around in a sea of emotional turbulence, from the very highs of praise and fan worship to the lows of critical reviews for a poor production or performance. Such turbulence is one of the chief reasons that actors and performers are often emotional messes or chaotic figures who cannot understand the swirling world of fan adulation, the fleeting nature of human fame, and the ultimate end that each human being naturally seeks. While the Oscar or Grammy may seem to be the endgame, if it were, why are so many in these industries in addictive or depressive states, prone to suicide rates higher than the general population and usually possessive of personal and family lives that can only be described as calamitous? Rock stars like Bruce Springsteen, James Taylor, Kurt Cobain—to name just a few—grapple with this inordinate adulation in human affairs and then find little peace or joy in the achievement, or at least are gasping from a sense of inadequacy. To be sure, it is harshly difficult to walk off stages where human adoration reaches levels beyond

[73] Dr. Robert Holden, "Ten Ways to Find Happiness," Oprah.com, accessed May 25, 2019, https://www.oprah.com/spirit/10-ways-to-find-happiness-dr-robert-holden.

normal human experience and then to encounter the segue into ordinary day-to-day life. In other words, it is a human high that can never be replicated, because it is neither normal nor consistent with the true nature of happiness. At its best, it is a temporary idol worship that leaves the actor craving more or hoping to avoid any future encounters. In his 2018 interview with *Esquire* magazine, Bruce Springsteen said:

> I had no inner peace whatsoever. And I said, "Gee, I really don't know. I don't know how long I could ..." It was a manic state, and it was just so profoundly emotionally and spiritually and physically uncomfortable that the only thing I've ever said was "Gee, I don't know, man ..." It gave me a little insight into ... Identity is a slippery thing no matter how long you've been at it. Parts of yourself can appear—like, whoa, who was *that* guy? Oh, he's in the car with everybody else, but he doesn't show his head too often, because he was so threatening to your stability. At the end of the day, identity is a construct we build to make ourselves feel at ease and at peace and reasonably stable in the world. But *being* is not a construct. Being is just being. In being, there's a whole variety of wild and untamed things that remain in us. You bump into those in the night, and you can scare yourself.[74]

These cases establish that happiness finds no home in the extremes of anything or any human person, that happiness yearns for equilibrium and balance rather than excess or defect in human

[74] Michael Hainey, "Beneath the Surface of Bruce Springsteen," Esquire.com, November 27, 2018, accessed May 25, 2019, https://www.esquire.com/entertainment/a25133821/bruce-springsteen-interview-netflix-broadway-2018.

affairs, and that a truly happy person seems to keep all things in their appropriate and proper context, fully understanding the joy that emerges from human activity but then ultimately comprehending that none of these events or conditions can substitute for our ultimate end. For both Aristotle and Aquinas, happiness cannot reside in human affairs alone but leads to the ultimate good, perfect good and Being, the transcendent reality that lacks nothing and needs nothing because of God's pure self-sufficiency. Only when we encounter this highest and most perfect form of Being will happiness be truly achieved. For Aristotle, this contemplative encounter and acknowledgment reaches a far less intimate conclusion than Aquinas, whose beatific or divine vision of God does the trick for perfect happiness, that any meaningful chance at real, unadulterated happiness, not subject to change or alteration, will depend on God. Everything else will come up short—although we may experience degrees and gradations of happiness in temporal experiences.

Aristotle

Some seem to think, not without reason, that the supreme good called happiness is a good belonging to this life. But this seems too superficial to be the good we are looking for.[75]

How nonsensical, if when a man is happy we may affirm it of him since [we] are unwilling to call the living happy on account of changes in the present life, because we think happiness permanent and not easily changeable, and because fortune often goes in cycles for the same persons.[76]

[75] *Nic. Ethics*, 1095b14–16; b23.
[76] *Nic. Ethics*, 1100a31; 1100b7.

Aquinas

Men think there is some happiness in this life because of a similarity of it to true happiness. They are not altogether wrong in so thinking.[77] Imperfect happiness which can be had in this life, can be lost.[78]

Now in this life all evil cannot be excluded. The present life is subject to many evils which cannot be avoided; the evil of ignorance on the part of the intellect; the evil of inordinate affection on the part of desire, and the evil of much suffering on the part of the body.[79]

Here both Aristotle and Aquinas lay out the very transitory nature of happiness in human life and especially how it can neither be sustained at a high energy level nor prevented from wane or correction due to the usual stresses of day-to-day life. No matter how you look at happiness in the long run, it is wise to keep its power and potential in a reasonable framework. Doing so assures a happier life where priorities make a bit more sense than those always craving the heights of exhilaration and joy. Looking to a higher order, to a divine realm where our Creator fashioned us as beings, will be the only true resting place in the matter of happiness. Charles Bruehl's wonderful text, *This Way Happiness*, explains why:

> The object to give man perfect happiness must itself be limitless. It must be the fullness of truth, goodness, beauty, and every conceivable perfection. This is God, who is the

[77] St. Thomas Aquinas, *Summa Theologica* [hereafter cited as *Summa*], I-II, q. 5, art. 3, ad.

[78] Aquinas, *Summa*, I-II, q. 5.

[79] Aquinas, *Summa*, I-II, q. 5. art. 3, corp.

> plenitude of being. In Him unalloyed happiness can be found.... With Him and all the good, man will live in a blessed community in which eternal harmony prevails and into which no disturbing shadow can fall, because it is centered on Him who is the source of all good, infinite, changeless, and everlasting. Perfect happiness will be ours when God, for whom we are made, becomes for us all in all.[80]

In the final analysis, that type of experience cannot really happen on this orb—maybe slivers of it or pieces of that experience, but perfect happiness while laudable is not achievable in this dimension. It awaits the next.

Happiness: Virtue and Vice

Aristotle

In every case the good of man will consist in action the best of his ability according to reason. In every case the good of man will consist in action conformable to virtue, and if there are a number of virtues, action conformable to the best and most perfect of them.[81]

Aquinas

Therefore, Happiness is obtained through works.... Happiness is the reward of works of virtue.[82]

[80] C. P. Bruehl, *This Way Happiness* (Milwaukee, WI: Bruce, 1941), 45.
[81] *Nic. Ethics*, 1098a7–18.
[82] Aquinas, *Summa*, I–II, q. 5, art. 7, sc.

The correlation between a virtuous life and disposition and human happiness is strongly advocated by both Aristotle and Aquinas. Happiness is "obtained through action," not mere desire.[83] The opposite conclusion, as to a vice-riddled life, is just as keenly deduced by these preeminent thinkers. In a nutshell, virtue and virtuous acts are consistent with our being and our essence and to constantly engage in virtuous activities leads to our flourishing and human development in accordance with our fundamental nature—a "moral excellence" that advances happiness in the human actor.[84] In being, we are what we are, whether human or animal in life, but our essence and our essential components are what make us that being precisely. So, for the being *Homo sapiens*, as the name implies, it is a being that thinks, or a being that is composed of mind, body, and spirit/soul.

Vice does the very opposite. Doing what is right and virtuous "brings happiness in its wake."[85] Human observation makes this quite plain, for the human actor who is temperate, courageous, generous and beneficent, prudential, driven by charity and love, strong and filled with fortitude, to name just a few attributes of virtue, tends to be a happier agent than his or her counterpart—the intemperate, stingy, fearful, impulsive and incoherent, hateful and vengeful, non-industrious, lazy, slothful, and promiscuous. This conclusion is not merely anecdotal but both quantitatively and qualitatively demonstrable. Much of the remainder of this text shall lay out the data and findings that strikingly manifest a correlation Aristotle and Aquinas made long before social and behavioral sciences with empirical data ever saw the light of day.

[83] Aquinas, *Summa*, I–II, q. 7, sc.

[84] *Nic. Ethics*, 1103a.

[85] Bruehl, *Happiness*, 37.

Hence, to have any reasonable chance at happiness, your decisions and choices as to behavior will have to be guided by virtue over vice. In fact, it would be difficult if not impossible to find any case where a vice-laden life was a happy life. The evidence overwhelmingly proves that drug addicts, prostitutes, promiscuously enslaved parties, and greedy hoarders of material goods and funds, as well as jealous and envious people, are never really happy. These attributes cannot, as Aristotle argues, produce any "state" conducive to happiness.[86]

Any evaluator of a life well lived always connects the examination to the question of virtue and vice. Virtuous people choose patterns of conduct that elevate the bulk of their personhood, that elevate the human spirit, the soul, and even the human body. When one tests and challenges oneself to be virtuous in all things, the demands are quite obvious and even more telling when compared to vice. For the vice-driven student is so lazy that studying is thrown to the wayside, or in other human interactions, when motivated by lust, hate, or vengeance, the end result is usually a very negative reality. The person operating in vice always chooses the easier path—to run in fear from injustice, to be envious of others rather than happy for their success and advancement, to hate rather than forgive. Vice gravitates to the lower common denominator while virtue aims to higher motives and purposes. However, our passions, our senses, and our drive toward pleasure sometimes make the choice of vice far easier than the choice of virtue. In virtue, there is limitation on human conduct, not the unbridled, unrestricted, and unregulated world of vice. This type of alleged "freedom" avoids the very idea of *moral excellence* because the choices made by the vice-ridden never

[86] *Nic. Ethics*, 1106a15.

lead to the type of contentment that happiness provides. Living in virtue, choosing the good, "is no easy task."[87] In all human action, choices can be made on either side of this virtue-vice continuum. Evaluate and compare both the choice of virtue and vice in table 2.1.[88]

A couple of observations are immediate. First, virtue is usually an act or activity discoverable in the mean between excessiveness and deficiency. In the *mean*, both Aristotle and Aquinas discover the proper formula for human action and human happiness. The mean is neither an algebraic formula nor geometric equation but a judgment as to how much conduct or lack thereof advances our state of happiness or personal peace. For example, the idea of temperance in sexual intercourse rests between complete promiscuity, where excessive and inordinate sexual action takes place, and intentional, nonreligious-based celibacy. In the middle of this spectrum one finds sexual intercourse with parameters, in marriage and with a partner one loves and is fully committed to. In this context, the happier party is the one, both Aristotle and Aquinas argue, that resides in the mean—the reasonable posture where sexuality has purpose and proper limitations, rather than those enslaved to sexual compulsion. The mean produces the greatest possible measure of human happiness. Of course, this is why prostitutes are not a very happy group and why these same people are so heavily involved in propping their state of happiness up with drugs and alcohol.

[87] *Nic. Ethics*, 1109a25.

[88] Aristotle, *The Ethics of Aristotle: The Nicomachean Ethics*, trans. J. K. Thomson (New York: Viking, 1955), 104, accessed May 25, 2019, https://www.cwu.edu/~warren/Unit1/aristotles_virtues_and_vices.htm.

Aristotle's Ethics: Table of Virtues and Vices

Sphere of Action or Feeling	Excess	Mean	Deficiency
Fear and Confidence	Rashness	Courage	Cowardice
Pleasure and Pain	Licentiousness/ Self-indulgence	Temperance	Insensibility
Getting and Spending (minor)	Prodigality	Liberality	Illiberality/ Meanness
Getting and Spending (major)	Vulgarity/ Tastelessness	Magnificence	Pettiness/ Stinginess
Honor and Dishonor (major)	Vanity	Magnanimity	Pusillanimity
Honor and Dishonor (minor)	Ambition/ Empty vanity	Proper ambition/ Pride	Unambitiousness/Undue humility
Anger	Irascibility	Patience/ Good temper	Lack of spirit/ Unirascibility
Self-expression	Boastfulness	Truthfulness	Understatement/ Mock modesty
Conversation	Buffoonery	Wittiness	Boorishness
Social Conduct	Obsequiousness	Friendliness	Cantankerousness
Shame	Shyness	Modesty	Shamelessness
Indignation	Envy	Righteous indignation	Malicious enjoyment/ Spitefulness

Table 2.1. Aristotle's Virtues and Vices.

Aristotle

There are three dispositions, of which two are vices: one by excess, the other by defect. The third is virtue and consists in the mean.[89]

Aquinas

Now it is clear that between excess and deficiency the mean is equality and conformity. Therefore it is evident that moral virtue observes the mean.[90]

On another level, it is really easy to see how people are fooled by the attractiveness of vice, especially as regards sensuality and pleasure as a driving principle. For in pleasure, especially the excessive variety, reason and intellect—of knowing good choices over bad ones—can be readily fooled by its stimulative alternative. The great Roman lawyer/philosopher Cicero called pleasure the "great imitator of truth," for those heavily hooked on any pleasure proposition convince themselves of the pleasure's inherent and sustainable goodness. Opioids illustrate this mirage of how pleasure rules rational beings and persons who really do know better. But once enslaved, there seems no way out, given the alternative. The sensual and appetitive buzz provided by the drugs consume the user in ways all inconsistent with a normal, happy life. The data on this artificial substitute for happiness and its corresponding destruction are stark and stunningly negative. See figure 2.1.[91]

89 *Nic. Ethics*, 1108b11–15.

90 Aquinas, *Summa*, I–II, q. 64, art. 1, corp.

91 CDC WONDER, "Overdose Death Rates," Centers for Disease Control and Prevention WONDER online database, December

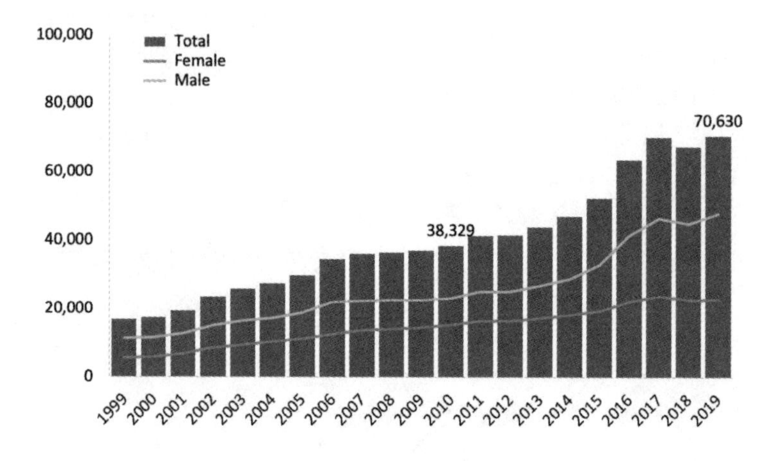

Figure 2.1. Increase in Opioid Overdoses since 1999.

Opioid usage does not even appear capable of achieving any "mean" usage despite its effective pain-killing capacity. Yet it is that very numbness and simultaneous "high" that draw so many into its capture, wittingly or not. Such usage cannot be described as virtuous. So widespread are the negative implications of its usage, and so obvious the user's understanding of the negative effects and ramifications, that users continue to choose otherwise. The national data cannot adequately describe the devastation that arises from this addictive vice. See figure 2.2.[92]

2020, accessed January 1, 2020, at https://www.drugabuse.gov/drug-topics/trends-statistics/overdose-death-rates.

[92] "What Is the U.S. Opioid Epidemic?" U.S. Department of Health and Human Services, accessed January 2, 2020, https://www.hhs.gov/opioids/about-the-epidemic/index.html.

THE OPIOID EPIDEMIC BY THE NUMBERS

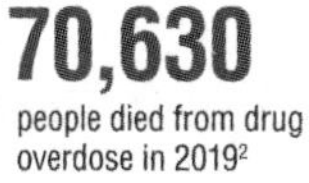

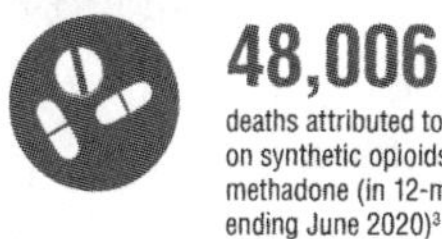

10.1 million
people misused prescription opioids in the past year[1]

2 million
people used methamphetamine in the past year[1]

50,000
people used heroin for the first time[1]

14,480
deaths attributed to overdosing on heroin (in 12-month period ending June 2020)[3]

SOURCES
1. 2019 National Survey on Drug Use and Health, 2020.

Figure 2.2. Opioid Statistics Are Mind-Numbing and Increasingly on the Rise.

And in the final analysis, aside from this behavior outside the mean of productive and virtuous human activity, opioid usage has caused an epidemic of deaths, victimizing those well aware of the potential and very terminal consequences. On top of all of this, how do happiness and human contentment thrive in such a horrid environment? The addict can never be at peace, since he or she is always craving, yearning, thirsting for, or obsessing over the next fix of drugs coursing through veins working beyond normal utility. The drug addict suffers from a cascade of malignant vices and conditions such as laziness and sloth, intellectual and physical stunting, sexually transmitted diseases (STDs) and medical infections beyond any normal profile, corrosive and deadly personal relationships, neglect and dereliction of parental and caregiver responsibility, and a general state that signifies at best a neutral state on the continuance of life. All in all, it is not a pretty picture, and to be certain, these conditions do not mirror the type of happiness and contentment consistent with a virtuous disposition.

Both Aristotle and Aquinas guarantee that a life not well lived, not in accordance with our basic nature and in conflict with what makes us flourish and grow as a human person, leads away from any happiness. To be sure, there will be ephemeral periods of pleasure-driven or -induced happiness—a false exhilaration that deceives its user into thinking that a feeling of this sort could not be all bad. And for that fleeting moment, the sensual and appetitive power of the human person dominates the thinking person, their intellect and brain, their reason and rationality.

The same could be said about pedophiles—yet more vice-ridden and unvirtuous people displaying no respect for the sanctity of children—in a behavior so abhorrent that it can never be measured by a mean or moderation. The only virtuous notion regarding this behavior is total avoidance. Pedophilia by its very nature is an extreme sexual excess that uses young and innocent children to gratify sexual desire. Completely and objectively a total vice, pedophilia drives a person toward some sensual gratification in place of a happiness that loves the good, the true, and all that is beautiful. Intellectually and rationally, the pedophile knows this but cannot control or corral the aberrant urges. Pedophiles, like drug addicts, have no peace, no contentment, no happiness, because the ends sought, the false goods pined for, lead to a markedly unhappy world. When the ultimate end of human existence is cast aside in favor of this temporary physical pleasure at the expense of an objectified child, the perpetrator cannot grasp onto any meaningful happiness.

Happiness finds its home in doing and living correctly, in conformity with our basic natures, and in adherence to what reason dictates and the proper ends and goods for the human person. Drug addiction, alcoholism, sexual addiction, lust, greed, and pedophilia, to name a few, drive the human player away from happiness and away from the human conduct that correctly resides in the mean. None of the characters exhibiting these traits shall ever be happy because none of these lifestyles are virtuous.

Happiness: The Goods and the Ends of a Self-Sufficient Life

Aristotle and Aquinas cannot guarantee much happiness to those neglecting the proper goods and ends for a life well lived. Hence, there are two questions that need analysis: First, what is a good and what goods are worth pursuing? Second, what is the end or purpose for human existence? While both are very weighty questions, each is a crucial element on the road to happiness. In the case of "goods," each thinker defines the term by its relationships with our own development and flourishing. In other words, what is good for us is what we ought to seek in every human activity. Hence, by way of example, health is for the good of the human person rather than sickness, for in health, the agent grows and flourishes.

Aristotle

Human good turns out to be activity of the soul in conformity with excellence, and if there are more than one excellence, in conformity with the best and most complete.[93]

Aquinas

Whereas virtue is a habit which is always referred to good ... so also is virtue called good, because by it something is good.[94]

Those who sin turn away from that in which their last end really consists: but they do not turn away from the intention of the last end, which intention they mistakenly seek in other things.[95]

For Aristotle and Aquinas, the array of goods is as myriad as the types of human activity. The unifier regarding all of them, whether it be art or architecture, music or gardening, carpentry or the playing of the lyre, is that the human person excels to the highest possible level in each and every activity. Living well, at the highest level of personal performance, will heavily depend on targeting the best in human action—not the tolerable or mediocre course of conduct but the most exceptional possibility or potentiality in human activity. All of this leads to a more complete and satisfying life; all of this elevates the human person to the greatest potential

[93] *Nic. Ethics*, 1098a15.

[94] Aquinas, *Summa*, I–II, q. 5, art. 4, ad 1.

[95] Aquinas, *Happiness*, 1.7.ad 1.

and actuality. Otherwise, the choice of the quasi-good—doing just enough to get by, shirking overall requirements and responsibilities, and being satisfied with a lesser rather than a greater good—drives to less happiness.

Achieving the highest heights in every human endeavor has a greater chance of ensuring appropriate goods chosen and directs us to our proper ends. And the most compelling end sought is happiness, for in the state of happiness the human agent moves closer to a more "complete and self-sufficient life."[96] Living a virtuous, moral, and upright life tends to advance the goods for our personhood and our community while the vice-driven actor becomes a hindrance to both self and those who are subjected to that vice. Think of the alcoholic and drug addict—the turmoil and sadness wreaked on family and friends and, even more compellingly, the loss and destruction of personal development. Few alcoholics and drug addicts, if any, achieve the goods necessary for a productive and happy life, and few elevate themselves toward any higher heights; instead, they dwell in the compulsion and obsession of a human activity that cannot lead to peace or contentment. All that remains is the drug or the drink, which in turn leads nowhere. On this score, Aquinas and Aristotle fully understand that one's choices to either good or evil, to virtue or vice, shape futures. All of it is very predictable.

Not surprisingly, there are those who claim these virtuous qualities that encompass a well-lived life are imposing draconian values; in some cases, critics of virtue theory argue that happiness is even possible without any morality, any moral sense, or decisions about conduct consistent with human flourishing. But this conclusion, according to Paul Bloomfield, is a fool's errand since the cheaters,

[96] *Nic. Ethics*, 1097b5–10.

the liars, the frauds who prey on others for their own advancement, "deceive themselves into believing otherwise, they know they do not deserve what they have ignobly attained."[97]

At another level, the quest for happiness, undertaken by a person fully cognizant of the goods to achieve that state, then becomes the "end" for all human existence. So, on the one hand, you must recognize the "goods" that advance you while, on the other hand, you need to appreciate that these very goods are tied and bound to any chance at happiness we might have. In the end, happiness is the end all of us seek.

Aristotle

Happiness, then, is something complete and self-sufficient, and is the end of action.[98]

Happiness then is the best, noblest, and most pleasant thing ... for all these properties belong to the best activities, and these, or one—the best—of these, we identify with happiness.[99]

What is best, what is superior and most perfect, and what is the most exceptional directly correlates to our degree or gradations of happiness. And since happiness is the "end" of every rational being, how does the human agent achieve the highest possible level of happiness? As we have already noted, none of that ambition is really possible, in the most complete sense, in the earthly world, for all human activity, while highly laudable, never achieves the

97 Bloomfield, "Morality," 2627.
98 *Nic. Ethics*, 1097b15–20.
99 *Nic. Ethics*, 1099a20–30.

perfection of the ultimate end, namely a divine good or Being. Even though Aristotle is a pagan, both he and Aquinas will reach similar, albeit theologically differing, conclusions on this question. For Aristotle, happiness, in its most perfect state, has to emanate or be part of a divine and fully perfect good. For Aquinas, it is the Beatific Vision of God—the joining of temporal man with an eternal God in the afterlife that is, has been, and will always be our ultimate end.

Aristotle

Clearly what applies to the best things is not praise, but something greater and better ... for what we do to the gods and the most godlike of men is to call them blessed and happy. And so too with good things; no one praises happiness as he does justice, but rather calls it blessed, as something more divine and better.[100]

Aquinas

Happiness is the attainment of the Perfect Good.... This can be proved again from the fact that man is capable of seeing God in which vision ... man's Perfect Happiness consists.[101]

Hence, until our passage from this earthly domain occurs, the quest for happiness shall be only partial yet very worthwhile. For in the final analysis, our encounter with God will not take place if

[100] *Nic. Ethics*, 1101b20–27.

[101] Aquinas, *Summa*, I–II, q. 5, art. 1, corp.

our human activity does not merit this eternal state of peace and contentment. In a way, this describes Heaven as Heaven may be, that achievement of pure, unadulterated happiness without want or need, or as already described, a state of perfect self-sufficiency, or as Aquinas describes, the "last end" that every human being seeks.[102] Only in this domain shall there be perfect happiness.

Summary

Before looking at more particular criteria for the attainment of happiness, this chapter laid out the foundational elements and definitions of what makes happiness possible according to Aquinas and Aristotle. From the outset of our examination, it is crucial to set forth reasonable expectations regarding happiness and to ensure that happiness is an attainable goal, although never a perfect reality while we are alive and kicking in the material world. Happiness has various levels and steps, ranging from the very imperfect version to the most perfect level before our God and Creator. It is crucial to know that from the beginning because our reasonableness on this score will lead to a happier life. No pill or therapy, no yoga or transcendental meditation, no psychoanalysis can ever lead to full, unbridled happiness, though it may help along the way for a few fleeting moments. Nor will social media, Facebook, Twitter, and the like lead to enduring happiness. In fact, recent studies have shown that social media and the phones that slavishly control online content are producing unexpected rates of unhappiness, and even suicide, in young people. Donna Feritas discovers this correlation in her text, *The Happiness Effect: How Social Media Is*

[102] Aquinas, *Summa*, I-II, q. 1, art. 7.

Driving a Generation to Appear Perfect at Any Cost.[103] Her fundamental conclusion is that a many young people are not concerned with being happy, only appearing happy.[104]

Aristotle and Aquinas provide a timeless formula for how to achieve a happy state. Aside from encouraging reasonable expectations as to its achievement while living in this world, both urge seekers of happiness to understand what it means to be happy. In place of a perpetual exhilaration and feeling of an endless emotional high, each urges that happiness be more a state of contentment, a condition of excellence, a mark of achievement at the very highest levels of potential, and the recognition that one has done all that can be done to be self-sufficient and worthy of praise in living the good life. That life consists of and encompasses every activity that can be described as virtuous, for happiness goes hand in hand with virtue while its opposite, vice, leads to another distressful and distraught destiny. The connection of virtue, in all its forms and categories, to the notion of happiness, is clearly one of the greatest contributions of Aristotle and Aquinas. For in this sense, happiness is within our grasp—rather than being an illusory and impossible state of being as we live out our daily existence. Making decisions and choices based on virtue, whether it be temperance, fortitude, charity, modesty, magnanimity, or courage, assuredly leads to greater levels of happiness than its counterpart in vice.

[103] Donna Feritas, *The Happiness Effect: How Social Media Is Driving a Generation to Appear Perfect at Any Cost* (London: Oxford University Press, 2017).

[104] Ibid. See also Alice G. Walton, "Phone Addiction Is Real—and So Are Its Mental Health Risks," Forbes.com, December 11, 2017, accessed May 25, 2019, https://www.forbes.com/sites/alicegwalton/2017/12/11/phone-addiction-is-real-and-so-are-its-mental-health-risks/#74f4342c13df.

Of course, making good decisions and being virtuous is to target and zero in on the "goods" that are conducive to human flourishing and growth—mentally, spiritually, and physically. What is a "good" should correlate to the activity undertaken. If the activity elevates us, develops us, by all means choose it, and all of these goods shall lead to happiness. At each stage in human existence, degrees of human happiness depend upon whether the activities we choose make happiness more or less likely. And since virtue is the barometer for happiness and vice the measure of sadness, there is a fighting chance to achieve the goal of happiness. At the last stage of our temporal existence, we are about to embark on a journey that makes perfect happiness a reality. In the afterlife, if we have lived well, in virtue, and tending to the goods consistent with human flourishing and development, we shall encounter our ultimate good and end—the God who fashioned us. Only here, only in this setting, both Aristotle and Aquinas agree, shall perfect happiness become a reality.

Rules for a Happy Life

2.0: That Happiness Is Unachievable in This World
2.1: That Happiness in This World Is Partial and Dependent on Choices
2.2: That Happiness Is Not Constant Exhilaration but a State of Contentment
2.3: That Happiness Depends on Virtue and the Virtuous Life
2.4: That Happiness Connects to Proper Goods and the End of Human Life
2.5: That Happiness Depends upon Human Flourishing and Development at the Highest Levels
2.6: That Happiness Resides in Our Ultimate End—God

3

Happiness: Wealth, Money, and Material Possessions

Introduction: Wealth and Human Activity

Aristotle

The excess vulgarity, lack of taste, and the like, which do not go to excess in the amount spent on right objects, but by showy expenditure in the wrong circumstances and the wrong manner.[105]

Aquinas

All things saleable can be had for money; not so for spiritual things, which cannot be sold.[106]

Whereas in the desire for wealth and for whatsoever temporal goods, the contrary is the case: for when we already possess them, we despise them and seek others.[107]

[105] *Nic. Ethics*, 1122a30.

[106] Aquinas, *Summa*, I–II, q. 2, art. 1, ad 2.

[107] Aquinas, *Summa*, I–II, q. 2, art. 1, ad.

The idea that money buys or assures happiness is a long-standing fable. Surely, one can readily conclude that money can and does provide economic security—freeing the human agent from the stresses and strains of having no money or wealth whatsoever. For most people, the choice between being poor and impoverished versus having some level of economic wealth is a no-brainer. To be lacking in the most basic material possessions, such as food and clothing, generally, outside of an aesthetic existence, does not generate large levels of happiness. Abject poverty usually leads to minimal levels of bliss and joy. However, a conscious decision to forego material goods and possessions because of service to others and any bona fide altruistic or charitable purpose can and does carve out a wondrous form of happiness. See figure 3.1.

Figure 3.1. President Ronald Reagan Presents Mother Teresa with the Presidential Medal of Freedom at a White House Ceremony as First Lady Nancy Reagan Looks On, June 20, 1985.

On the other hand, extreme wealth and material largesse may do little to elevate the happiness barometer for most human beings. Recent research at Purdue University seems to indicate that wealth beyond $100,000 trends away from happiness more than leans toward it.

Princeton University's comprehensive study on wealth and well-being targets the ideal salary of $75,000 as a benchmark for emotional contentment.[108] Other studies show that the economic quality of life improves with money although one's subjective well-being may be less positive than those with less. The National Academy of Sciences confirms this finding but demonstrates a drop-off in emotional and personal well-being as income levels rise. See figure 3.2.[109]

A recent study conducted by the University of Pennsylvania's Wharton School of Business does find a happiness correlation derived from being wealthier rather than poor.[110] Wealth and money may eliminate certain stresses but at the same time generate other stresses that lead to less happiness. The key will be finding the mean of wealth, so to speak. The world is filled with many examples of how money fails to buy love, affection, real friendship, or any meaningful happiness. For this and many other reasons, wealth shall never fill that natural need for a meaningful life and a true sense of well-being. Wealth may bring some temporary and

[108] D. Daniel Kahneman and Angus Deaton, "High Income Improves Evaluation of Life but Not Emotional Well-Being," *Proceedings of the National Academy of Sciences USA* 107, no. 38 (September 2010): 16489–16493, accessed May 25, 2019, https://www.pnas.org/doi/10.1073/pnas.1011492107.

[109] Ibid., https://www.pnas.org/content/107/38/16489/tab-figures-data.

[110] Michele W. Berger, "Money Matters to Happiness—Perhaps More Than Previously Thought," *PennToday*, January 18, 2021, accessed January 1, 2022, at https://penntoday.upenn.edu/news/money-matters-to-happiness-perhaps-more-than-previously-thought.

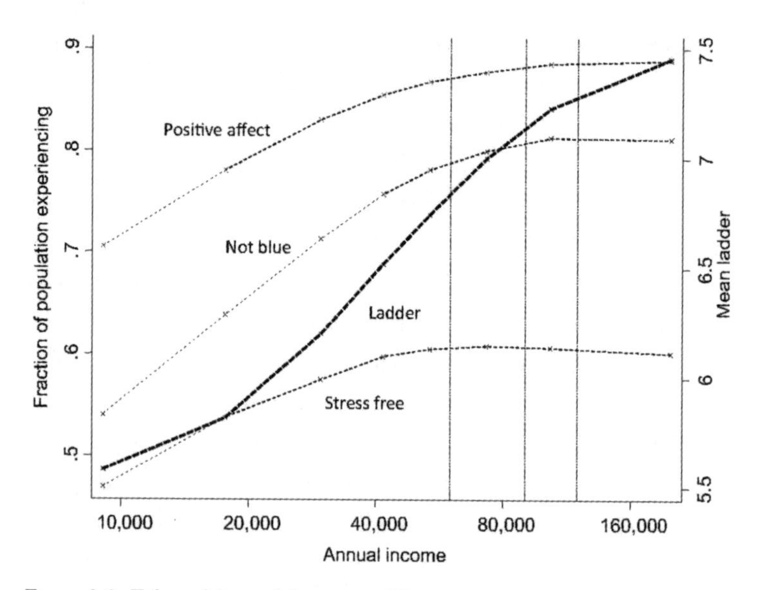

Figure 3.2. Effect of Annual Income on Happiness.

fleeting happiness but nothing so stable and dependable as the higher order of things is capable of, for only when we recognize the source of real happiness is our Creator will we be "free from torturing restlessness."[111] Rather than this recognition, the world too often encounters high levels of tragedy in the rich and famous whose purpose and aim reside solely in the here and now.

This is especially the case of those who generationally inherit wealth, who are rich upon birth, so to speak. For many of those born into wealth, the will to succeed is generally very soft; the incentive to excel is replaced by a comfortable laziness and a person's usual ambition replaced with an attitude of "too much too soon."[112] As

[111] Bruehl, *This Way Happiness*, 182.

[112] Deborah L. Jacobs, "Why Family Wealth Is a Curse," Forbes.com, March 1, 2013, accessed May 25, 2019, https://www.forbes.

heir to the Georgia-Pacific fortune, Thayer Willis describes this overall mental state:

> The biggest curse of intergenerational wealth for me and many other people is the illusion that you don't have to do much with your life. You might want to and you might make the effort, but you don't have the same pressure to earn enough to live on. And that takes away a lot of the incentive to find meaningful work.[113]

In addition to this general indifference, there is a subliminal ingratitude and cavalier attitude toward the blessings that wealth might and often does provide—an incapacity to really appreciate the station and security that wealth brings, and even more compellingly a refusal to put that same wealth to good use.

It is a story told and retold many times, from the Kennedy dynasty[114] to the oil baron John Paul Getty, with the family and its descendants often suffering from extraordinary levels of tragedy and corresponding unhappiness.[115]

Oil tycoon John Paul Getty amassed wealth at levels almost incalculable, yet he suffered through so many tragedies and sad events that one wonders if the wealth ever really made any positive

---

com/sites/deborahljacobs/2013/03/01/why-family-wealth-is-a-curse/#3bc2f9287887.

113 Ibid.

114 For a compelling timeline of the various tragedies that have haunted the Kennedy family, visit https://www.infoplease.com/timeline-kennedy-tragedies.

115 For a look at the Johnson & Johnson family wealth and corresponding tragedy, see Emma Garman, "Behind the Johnson & Johnson Curse," *Daily Beast*, August 11, 2013, accessed May 25, 2019, https://www.thedailybeast.com/behind-the-johnson-and-johnson-curse.

difference in his life.[116] Indeed, excessive wealth may have led to the day-to-day tragedy that became normative.

In the sports world, to further edify this lack of happiness, the bulk of athletes in the National Basketball Association, the National Football League, and the National Hockey League, at some point, even though the majority garner exceptional amounts of cash and salary, experience bankruptcy and money difficulties soon after retirement. The data and empirical research compellingly demonstrate this very bleak economic reality.[117]

Hence, the correlation between wealth amassed and wealth retained can be tenuous and fleeting, and if wisely and prudently managed, these funds would not simply evaporate into thin air. But this is precisely what happens so regularly, because these athletes value wealth and money for reasons that are so extreme that its future preservation remains almost impossible. Driven by compulsion, impulse buying, sale and exchange for its own sake, investing in questionable schemes and the people behind them to horde even more money, hoodwinked and swindled by alleged "financial advisers," the once rich in wealth and material descend into another version of poverty once never thought possible.

If these cases illustrate anything, especially given the astronomical sums at stake, it is that money cannot and does not buy peace

[116] For a full accounting of the story, see Tami Abdollah and John Rogers, "Getty Oil Heir's Death Latest in String of Family Tragedies," *Pittsburgh Post-Gazette*, April 2, 2015, https://www.post-gazette.com/business/powersource/2015/04/02/Getty-oil-heir-s-death-latest-in-string-of-family-tragedies-2/stories/201504020155.

[117] For a compelling discussion, see Pablo S. Torre, "How (and Why) Athletes go Broke," Sports Illustrated Vault, March 23, 2009, accessed May 25, 2019, https://www.si.com/vault/2009/03/23/105789480/how-and-why-athletes-go-broke.

or tranquility and does not assure the type of happiness that either Aristotle or Aquinas advances. For money and material worth are meaningless, in and of themselves, especially if the person entrusted with this wealth lacks the discipline and virtuous disposition to manage said funds. In this way, Aristotle and Aquinas see wealth as a means to a more secure life but never as the ultimate or primordial end in human operations, or for that matter an end that should be obsessively pursued. As in all things, both thinkers call upon the human agent to live in the mean of wealth and material goods— in the moderation of activity rather than in its excess or defect. Bruehl comments, "On the other side of the ocean, excessive, unbridled wealth can lead its possessor to an almost compulsive, obsessive desire to mass more wealth on top of incalculable wealth, for nothing 'enslaves men than the desire for riches.'"[118]

At the same time, neither Aristotle nor Aquinas is opposed to wealth or finds its possession inconsistent with a virtuous life, unless the possessor becomes stingy, miserly, prodigal or wasteful, and excessively enslaved to its pursuit. For in wealth, like all other human action, there is a balance to be achieved—a mean and moderation that makes wealth a most excellent thing.

Happiness, Wealth, and the Virtuous Life

Given all of this, it is clear that money and wealth cannot and does not buy happiness, although as one commentator remarked, money and wealth "may be a case of preventing sadness more than buying happiness."[119] The research also indicates that it is not wealth for

[118] Bruehl, *Happiness*, 182.

[119] "Money and Economics: The Surprising Research," Prosperity Economics, accessed July 6, 2022, https://prosperityeconomics.org/money-and-happiness/.

its own sake or possession that will elevate one's spirits or make a person contented, but more that the funds are being used for good and noble purposes, both personally and collectively. Since money is a means to an end, not the perfect good or end we seek, it can never fully satisfy. By contrast, however, some suggest that an alternative focus on charitable giving, doing good works, or expressions of gratitude may lead to a happier state more readily than simple ownership.[120]

Aristotle

> The life of money-making is one undertaken under compulsion, and is evidently not the good we are seeking; for it is merely useful and for the sake of something else.[121]

Aquinas

> All material things obey money, so far as the multitude of fools is concerned, who know no other than material goods.... But we should take our estimation of human goods not from the foolish but from the wise.[122]

Money and wealth, therefore, are tools for the living rather than the ultimate aim for human existence and are more properly described as a mechanism that makes possible not only necessities

[120] Emily L. Polak and Michael E. McCollough, "Is Gratitude an Alternative to Materialism?," *Journal of Happiness Studies* 7, no. 3 (September 2006): 343–360.

[121] *Nic. Ethics*, 1096a1–10.

[122] Aquinas, *Summa*, I–II, q. 2, art. 1, ad 1.

for human life but also a degree of delight and enjoyment. Even so, in and of itself, money cannot deliver the type of happiness that those enslaved by money often yearn for. Money is merely an attachment to that person rather than part of his or her essential makeup or purpose. No amount of money will produce happiness if the human person resists or rejects a virtuous and good pattern of human choices. To live in virtue assures that the money in one's possession will be used prudently, sagaciously, and temperately, as well as for the benefit of others rather than exclusively for self. Consider the plight of large lottery winners—a group that everyone invariably seems to envy as having conquered life's needs, wants, and corresponding hopes. Yet research into lottery winners does not paint a pretty picture of eventual tranquility, or even economic stability and surety of the remainder of one's life. Some studies indicate that nearly one-third of all lottery winners find themselves broke and bankrupt a short time after collecting large winnings.[123] Another study demonstrated that windfall sums of money, whether by lottery or large inheritance, are not valued in the same way as earned income, and hence are subject to patterns of spending and use far less concerned about conservation and more likely extravagant expenditure. The end result is smaller portions of these winnings are preserved for long-term financial security.[124]

[123] See Ric Edelman, "Why So Many Lottery Winners Go Broke," Fortune, January 15, 2016, accessed May 25, 2019, https://fortune.com/2016/01/15/powerball-lottery-winners/. See also Jay L. Zagorsky, "You Can Win a Billion and Still Go Bankrupt," BBC Capital, October 25, 2018, accessed May 25, 2019, http://www.bbc.com/capital/story/20181024-you-can-win-a-billion-and-go-bankrupt.

[124] See Guido W. Imbens, Donald B. Rubin, and Bruce Sacerdote, "Estimating the Effect of Unearned Income on Labor Earnings, Savings, and Consumption: Evidence from a Survey of Lottery

Most analysis seems to hold that the money by itself does less to advance happiness as much as the wise use of said funds and the even wiser saving and preservation of those funds. Avoiding scams and predatory people goes a long way in this situation too.

On the other hand, some studies conclude that winning large sums of money can lead to greater life satisfaction or happier results than continuous losing.[125] However, these findings speak of "life satisfaction" that the University of Stockholm concluded should not be equated with the term *happiness* in the analysis of lottery winners. Satisfaction implies opportunity to live more fully, to do more since one has the capacity to undertake more, and to live a life filled with more experiences. But the question of whether or not this level or type of activity can be defined as the tranquility and contentment of happiness is really debatable.[126]

Other studies show that while wealth and material possessions may lead to greater security in human affairs, the amassing of wealth for its own sake is generally a dead-end street, or at least leads to a sense of incompleteness. An exclusive focus on material possession in an obsessive sense "ultimately undermines the search for happiness and psychological fulfillment."[127] On top of this,

---

Players," *American Economic Review* 91, no. 4 (September 2001): 778–794.

[125] Erik Lindqvist, Robert Östling, and David Cesarini, "Long-Run Effects of Lottery Wealth on Psychological Well-Being," *National Bureau of Economic Research Working Paper* 24667 (May 2018), accessed May 25, 2019, https://www.nber.org/papers/w24667.

[126] See Erik Lindqvist, "Does Winning the Lottery Make You Happier?," Stockholm University, November 23, 2018, accessed May 25, 2019, https://www.su.se/english/research/does-winning-the-lottery-make-you-happier-1.414151.

[127] Polak and McCollough, "Gratitude," 344.

the problem of money and wealth cannot be separated from the quality of the person and the character of the money's possessor. Give bad, undisciplined people large sums of money, and those funds, as a result of free choice, will be directed toward bad and unproductive activities. In other words, the money mirrors the character of its possessor and the virtue or vices of that person who has control over it. So the virtuous person, the industrious, the generous, the wise and prudent and self-disciplined person, is less likely to squander the assets as much as the vice-consumed party. A recent study by MIT in its journal *The Review of Economics and Statistics* concluded that "a comparison of Florida Lottery winners who randomly received $50,000 to $150,000 to small winners indicates that such transfers only postpone bankruptcy rather than prevent it."[128] The wealth itself cannot control the human agent although the personal character and overall disposition of its possessor clearly does.

In thc final analysis, it is impossible to separate the destiny of money and wealth from the destiny of human choice in day-to-day affairs. For this reason, the irresponsible party achieving wealth, whether by lottery, professional sports contracts, inheritance, or other means, will use those funds as irresponsibly as in other facets of their lives. When St. Thomas speaks of "fools" this is precisely what he means—that money cannot change a fool into being wise, or vice versa for that matter—at least in most cases. For Aristotle, the central question becomes the character of one's life

[128] See Scott Hankins, Mark Hoekstra, and Paige Marta Skiba, "The Ticket to Easy Street? The Financial Consequences of Winning the Lottery," *The Review of Economics and Statistics* 93, no. 3 (2011): 961–969, accessed March 1, 2019, https://direct.mit.edu/rest/article-abstract/93/3/961/57969/The-Ticket-to-Easy-Street-The-Financial?redirectedFrom=fulltext.

that money and wealth cannot subvert if truly attentive to a virtuous life. Living a virtuous, well-ordered, and more self-sufficient lifestyle, one that values proper goods and ends for the human person, is a better guarantor of happiness than the mere amassing of material goods or currency.

Aristotle

> No blessed man can become miserable, for he will never do the acts that are hateful and mean. For the man who is truly good and wise, we think, bears all the chances of life becomingly and always makes the best of circumstances.[129]

Aquinas

> It is impossible for man's happiness to consist in wealth.[130]

Contemporary research has increasingly shown that generosity with wealth—its usage for the benefits of others in need—is a stronger promoter of personal happiness than wealth's ownership alone. When money is all about self, to the exclusion of those truly in bona fide need, the happiness quotient shall be lower than when the wealthy owner finds a way to disburse in charity. Here too, we see how living in virtue, with a charitable disposition and a meaningful love of our neighbors, to aid and assist truly worthy causes with these funds, leads to greater levels of happiness. Charity, of course, is the greatest of all virtues, and when used appropriately, the grant or giving

[129] *Nic. Ethics*, 1100b1–5.

[130] Aquinas, *Summa*, I–II, q. 2, art. 1.

of large sums of money to worthy individuals or causes will lead to greater levels of happiness than money's mere hoarding and control.

Charitable giving should not be without plan or merit but is instead focused upon worthy targets and plausible activities that bring measurable change. Thus, it would make little if any sense to give millions to homeless people on the street, but far greater sense to reward the Salvation Army or Catholic Charities, entities that funnel funds wisely and in proper discretion. Good works are fostered by these funds, and one's self-worth and vision, because of this generosity, remain both positive and continuous. A recent study by the University of Chicago and Northwestern University concludes that the joy and happiness relating to charitable giving appears to be long-lasting no matter the repetition in giving, especially when compared to "funding" one's own self-interest.[131]

Jenny Santi's *Giving Way to Happiness* dedicates an entire book to the benefits and positive happiness that arise from a life of giving and charitable donations. It is a work clearly worth the read.[132] What Jenny Santi lays out are the many, many benefits from living and giving in charity, in love and care of others worthy of our attention. Both Aristotle and St. Thomas reached these very same conclusions centuries ago. In Aristotle, the idea of charity was encompassed in the virtues of liberality and generosity—that mean between the giving and keeping of wealth. For St. Thomas the stress was on Christian charity as a theological virtue, which expects natural generosity to those in need. It is a Christian obligation to

[131] Ed O'Brien and Samantha Kassirer, "People Are Slow to Adapt to the Warm Glow of Giving," *Psychological Science* 30, no. 2 (2019): 193–204, accessed March 1, 2019, https://journals.sagepub.com/doi/full/10.1177/0956797618814145.

[132] Jenny Santi, *The Giving Way to Happiness* (New York: TarcherPerigee, 2016).

care for our neighbor. Just as compellingly, St. Thomas sees charity as the base and foundation for every other virtue. Without charity, all other virtuous activity is impossible.

Aristotle

Now spending and giving seem to be the using of wealth; taking and keeping rather the possession of it. Hence it is the mark of the liberal man to give to the right people than to take from the right sources and not to take from the wrong. For it is the characteristic of excellence to do good than have good done to one.[133]

Aquinas

Now the proper object of love is the good; so that wherever there is a special aspect of good, there is a special kind of love. But the Divine good, inasmuch as it is the object of happiness, has a special aspect of good, wherefore the love of charity, which is the love of that good, is a special kind of love. Therefore charity is a special virtue.[134]

Happiness, Levels of Wealth, and Justice

Obvious to any observer are the distinct and very differing levels of wealth, money, and material possessions. In the modern political climate, the differences are often labeled the "haves" and the

[133] *Nic. Ethics*, 1120a1–15.

[134] Aquinas, *Summa*, II-II, q. 23, art. 4, corp.

"have-nots," and in the latter instance, there subsequently occurs an immediate, almost knee-jerk reaction that the differences are a sign of the world's injustice and lack of care. Yet this conclusion, often posed by those leaning left or socialist, could not be more incorrect. For the question of justice in economic distribution can never be a mathematical equality—always the same for everyone and everybody. That sort of distribution is bound to lead to an unjust society far more quickly than a just one, according to both Aristotle and St. Thomas. Communism and socialism have proven that repeatedly, despite what a growing crop of politicos advocate by calling for redistribution to reparations. Quick visits to Cuba, North Korea, and present-day Venezuela illustrate and edify the ravages caused by this obsession with economic sameness and equality. These countries are far from the idyllic paradises the socialists and communists promise. See table 3.1.[135]

Name	Population 2021	Population 2020	Growth Rate
China	1,444,216,107	1,439,323,776	0.34%
Vietnam	98,168,833	97,338,579	0.85%
North Korea	25,887,041	25,778,816	0.42%
Cuba	11,317,505	11,326,616	-0.08%
Laos	7,379,358	7,275,560	1.43%

Table 3.1. Population Growth Rates.

[135] "Total Population by Country 2022," World Population Review, accessed January 1, 2022, http://worldpopulationreview.com/countries.

Other countries, while not full-fledged communist operations, adopt socialist policies that favor all sorts of economic redistribution, a reality currently even advocated in the American Republic by a new crop of politicos big on promises and—like the rest of the group—short on delivery. If intentions paved the way for collective wealth, the experiments in both communism and socialism might, by now, have yielded some fruit. However, these ideologies, allegedly rooted in justice, produce the very opposite results because the model runs contrary to how human beings are wired.

While the idea might be laudable, the end results of a socialist dream always turn into the worst nightmare. The reason for this is very simple: equal distribution fails to reflect the differing talents and abilities of citizens; fails to account for degrees of effort and energy among the whole range of citizenry; and, by every measure, stunts human initiative and inventiveness. If everyone gets the same, why bother? For the medical doctor in Cuba, who makes sixty-two dollars a month, cannot be of the same professional acumen as the heart specialists at Sloan-Kettering in New York, for there really is no motivation to be at one's most excellent. Think of a baseball team. If a player bats .385 and another .121, and both receive the same compensation, why excel in performance? What difference does it make? In both of these instances we encounter the idea of justice, both economic and personal. For in both Aristotle and Thomas, justice is about what one is "due"—what one is really worth compared to others and how some people deservedly make more than others. A janitor, while carrying out honorable and laudable work, is not a nuclear engineer, a teacher, or a heart surgeon, and it would be unjust if the same compensation be paid for work that calls for higher levels of preparation and investment. Just as importantly, Aristotle and Aquinas urged that property rights and proprietary interests be privately owned rather than follow a government-controlled state socialist model.[136]

Private ownership promotes direct, individual interest in property and rewards those who take risks in said property or who toil for its betterment.[137] Private ownership ties to human motivation and incentive rather than the drab world of uniformity, despite effort and energy expended. Anyone who has ever worked in an environment where everyone gets the same no matter the level of effort—a charge often leveled against excessive forms of unionism and protectionism—can understand how demoralizing the equal formula of economic justice can be. Those same debates can be heard about the elimination of private health insurance with the replacement being a single-payer governmental system. See figure 3.3.

Common sense dictates that those who compete against one another, namely medical insurers and providers, are bound to produce a better result than a governmentally orchestrated health program of singular choice. That experiment has already been tested in Cuba, Angola, England, and other countries, who see their single-payer system suffering from long waits and a lack of choices in every context of the medical complex.

In the eyes of Aristotle and Aquinas, nothing so universal and singular could ever be the best and most just result. Justice demands excellence. Justice is not sameness but proportionality but depends upon the investment of time and energy of the medical providers as with any other human activity.

[136] See Aristotle, *Politics* [hereafter cited as *Pol.*], 1263–1264. See also Hermann Chroust and Robert J. Affeldt, "The Problem of Private Property according to St. Thomas Aquinas," *Marquette Law Review* 34, no. 3 (1950–1951): 151, accessed March 1, 2019, http://scholarship.law.marquette.edu/mulr/vol34/iss3/2.

[137] *Nic. Ethics*, 1130b1–5; Aquinas, *Summa*, II–II, q. 66, art. 2, ad 1.

Figure 3.3. Congresswoman Alexandria Ocasio-Cortez of New York, Advocate for Single-Payer Health System, the "Green New Deal," and Free College, Is Unabashedly a Democratic Socialist.

Aristotle

This form of justice, then is complete excellence. And it is complete excellence in its fullest sense, because it is the actual exercise of complete excellence. It is complete because he who possesses it can exercise excellence towards others too and not merely by himself.[138]

Property should be in a certain sense common, but, as a general rule, private; for, when everyone has a distinct interest, men will not complain of one another, and they will make more progress, because everyone will be attending to his own business.[139]

[138] *Nic. Ethics*, 1129b25–30.

[139] *Pol.*, 1163b25–30.

Aquinas

First, because every man is more careful to procure what is for him alone than that which is common to many or to all: since each one would shirk the labor and leave to another that which concerns the community. Secondly, because human affairs are conducted in a more orderly fashion if each man is charged with taking care of some particular things himself, whereas there would be confusion if everyone had to look after any one thing indeterminately. Thirdly, because a more peaceful state is ensured to man if each one is contended with his own.[140]

Hence, the virtue of justice is advanced when wealth and material goods are not commonly owned, but distinctly and individually cared for. A just society is more likely when individuals connect their own efforts and investment to their own self-interest. Therefore, there is no automatic vice in the personal amassing of wealth, as long as done in justice to others and the community itself. In fact, Aristotle and Aquinas directly and unequivocally connect the collection and maintenance of wealth with a life well lived—justly and charitably lived within the context of both self and the larger community. In contrast, the communist ideal of Stalin, Chairman Mao, Pol Pot, Fidel Castro, and the like stripped away individual ownership and tore down the natural instincts to oversee and care for what a person owns and is responsible for. For this and a host of other reasons, communist societies are not only poor materially; since they are incapable of producing goods and services at the level

[140] Aquinas, *Summa*, II–II, q. 66, art. 2.

any capitalist society is capable of, these governmental forms are universally unjust in the care of the citizenry. Few would or even could argue that communism and socialism have been bastions of freedom and productivity. In fact, despite what some modern politicos are bandying about, the record of these governmental structures is uniformly and universally bleak. On the other hand, countries that promote self-worth and human initiative appear more successful in developing more contented populations. Some have attempted to categorize countries on a continuum of happiness by developing a list of countries that appear to be or are the happiest. While some countries may offer up certain benefits, like health care, the happiest countries are not socialist or communist operations. A recent list of the happiest countries demonstrates how democracies or republics seem to produce the best results for its citizenry. While the United States comes in twenty-third out of 178 nations, the ten happiest countries are:

1. Denmark
2. Switzerland
3. Austria
4. Iceland
5. The Bahamas
6. Finland
7. Sweden
8. Bhutan
9. Brunei
10. Canada[141]

Analysis as to why these countries promote the greatest levels of happiness, according to social psychologist Adrian White of the University of Leicester, depends on three variables: health, wealth, and education.[142] Of course, there is really no perfect way to measure the happiness of a state or country, but it is fair to conclude these nations are freer than their communist and socialist counterparts,

[141] "Economics: The Well-Being of Nations," *The Futurist*, November–December 2006, 12.

[142] Ibid., 12.

where happiness generally takes a dive. Other studies have shown that happiness cannot be exclusively tied to wealth and economic prosperity. Just as critical is how a nation-state provides for its people in a social and a psychological sense—in other words, how prosperous are its settings for play, for research, for family activities, and for the overall conditions to enjoy the world around each citizen. This is less a material concern than it is a cultural condition where happiness can flourish. In contrast, it is difficult to envision a happy state in a Gulag or locked-down society allowing no expression of ideas, whether it be art or music, travel or cultural opportunities. Again, none of this is perfect science, but a recent study in the *Journal of Personality and Social Psychology* makes plain that money alone will not assure a happy life. "Our findings indicate that more than money [is required] for a quality of life ... this means that societies must pay careful attention to social and psychological variables, not simply to enlarging their economies."[143] See figure 3.4.[144]

Conclusion: The Balance of Wealth and Virtue Leads to Happiness

If individuals conclude that money buys happiness, they will be sorely disappointed. And while being impoverished, outside some altruistic vow, is not a state conducive to happiness, neither does having too much guarantee human happiness. In fact, our analysis of empirical studies on the range of funds necessary for a happy life

[143] Ed Diener et al., "Wealth and Happiness across the World: Material Prosperity Predicts Life Evaluation, Whereas Psychological Prosperity Predicts Positive Feeling," *Journal of Personality and Social Psychology* 99, no. 1 (2010): 61.

[144] "About Bernie," accessed May 25, 2019, https://www.sanders.senate.gov/about.

Figure 3.4. Senator Bernie Sanders, Avowed Democratic Socialist.

shows a monetary amount neither in excess nor in deficit but, as always posed by Aquinas and Aristotle, in the mean and sensible.

In addition, wealth must always be coupled with virtue to assure its proper usage, maintenance, and preservation. Wealth and virtue balance one another and assure that monetary resources be employed to better one's life and the community that surrounds us. Wealth must be dealt with in justice, in charity, and in prudence.

Finally, the question of happiness and wealth is both an individual and collective reality and inevitably must weave its way back to the governmental form imposed on the citizenry. Free societies that value private ownership and a system of rewards and incentives for those who show the greatest ambition and incentive, for those who live in accordance with justice and charity, produce happier populations. Repressive governmental forms that crush human initiative by the excessive oversight and taking of wealth for redistribution are not models for collective happiness. Our list of communist nations attests to this stark difference from free market countries. To illustrate, it is a safe bet to argue that the populace of Venezuela is not a happy lot as it suffers under the tyranny and socialistic failure of the current president, Nicolás Maduro.

Aside from a collapsing health-care and economic system, food shortages, and a hunger crisis, the bulk of its population even lacks basic necessities like soap and toilet paper. Even though its oil reserves are almost unrivaled, the entire production system, since it has been nationalized under socialist policies, no longer has its once vaunted capacity to generate wealth.[145] The entire population has suffered staggering weight losses to the point of abject hunger while at the same time what foodstuffs are available are subject to massive hyperinflation. Under any reasonable standard, these conditions cannot be a recipe for happiness for the nation-state and its inhabitants. The collective misery of the Venezuelan people does not arise because the government governs justly and virtuously.

At the same time, those in authority horde cash at the expense of those truly in need and bypass the most basic requirements of Christian charity. Venezuela illustrates that need for balance between the acquisition of wealth and the virtuous life. Having too much and having nothing cannot generate the peace, the contentment and tranquility that being self-sufficient affords the free person. And while Venezuela is not the only country that illustrates this very negative reality, it is a very telling piece of the wealth puzzle, a graphic example of how happiness cannot abandon virtue. For when the citizens and leaders live in accordance with

[145] See Antoine Halff et al., "Apocalypse Now: Venezuela, Oil and Reconstruction," Columbia Global Energy Dialogues, accessed May 25, 2019, https://growthlab.cid.harvard.edu/files/growthlab/files/cgepapocalypsenowvenezuelaoilandreconstruction7_17_1.pdf.

virtue, when each understands that wealth in and of itself can never really bring true and unbridled happiness because that only emerges when God or the divine good remains our ultimate end, and when the citizen and the system itself reward the industrious and the lawful citizens trying to do the right thing in all of their activity, only then will happiness become possible.

Rules for a Happy Life

3.0: That Happiness Cannot Be Solely Derived from Money

3.1: That Happiness Cannot Be Solely Derived from Material Possessions

3.2: That Happiness Is Less Likely in Poverty, Deprivation, and Impoverishment

3.3: That Happiness Does Not Occur in Equal Distribution or Communal Sharing of Property

3.4: That Happiness in Matters of Wealth, Money, and Possessions Needs a Virtuous Disposition

3.5: That Happiness Depends on a Proper Balance of "Having" and "Giving"

3.6: That Happiness Depends on Private Ambition and Private Ownership Rather Than Collective Distribution

3.7: That Happiness Is Not Assured Even When the Economic Quality of Life Is Highly Prosperous

3.8: That Happiness and the Vice of Greed Are Utterly Incompatible

3.9: That Happiness and the Virtue of Charity Are Completely Compatible

4

Happiness: Fame, Power, and Honor

Introduction: Do Fame and Honor Bring True Happiness?

Aristotle

Happiness, then, is something complete and self-sufficient, and is the end of action. [Fame] we choose for the sake of happiness.[146]

Aquinas

Fame has no stability; in fact, it is easily ruined by false report. And if sometimes it endures, this is by accident. But happiness endures of itself, and forever.[147]

The idea that happiness emerges from fame, honor, power, and glory over the course of human history is fiction that so many buy into. Consider the entertainment world—filled with people who, for

[146] *Nic. Ethics*, 1097b1–30.

[147] Aquinas, *Summa*, I–II, q. 2, art. 3, ad 3.

good or bad reason, pine for success in their fields, whether acting, music, art, or dance, and are driven to be excellent at their craft. And to be sure, history also demonstrates that there are honorable and very virtuous actors, politicians, and other famous people. However, the evidence, both anecdotally and empirically, paints a troubled picture of exception rather than the rule for so many who have achieved fame. Others might hope for this notoriety because at least someone is paying attention to what they are doing. For it is common knowledge that many entertainers suffer emotional deficits in childhood, trauma, or turbulence in their upbringing, and that these negative conditions will be softened by the acquisition of fame.[148]

Most people on a quest for fame and glory often assume that happiness will follow because the depth and breadth of that fame, and often corresponding fortune, will be enough to overcome any personal or familial deficits. In the world of musical entertainment, especially rap, heavy metal, and rock and roll, the price of fame equates with higher rates of accidental death, suicide, and homicidal death than the general population. The differences are stark, according to Dianna Theadora Kenny, professor of psychology and music at the University of Sydney, who concludes that the life expectancy of both male and female pop musicians is, on average, twenty years less than your average individual. See figure 4.1.[149]

[148] For a fascinating study on this motivation for being famous in entertainment or politics, see D. Aberbach, *Charisma in Politics, Religion, and the Media: Private Trauma, Public Ideals* (Basingstoke: Palgrave Macmillan UK, 1996).

[149] Dianna Theadora Kenny, "Stairway to Hell: Life and Death in the Pop Music Industry," *The Conversation*, October 26, 2014, accessed May 25, 2019, http://theconversation.com/stairway-to-hell-life-and-death-in-the-pop-music-industry-32735. Dianna Theadora Kenny is a professor of psychology and music at the University of Sydney.

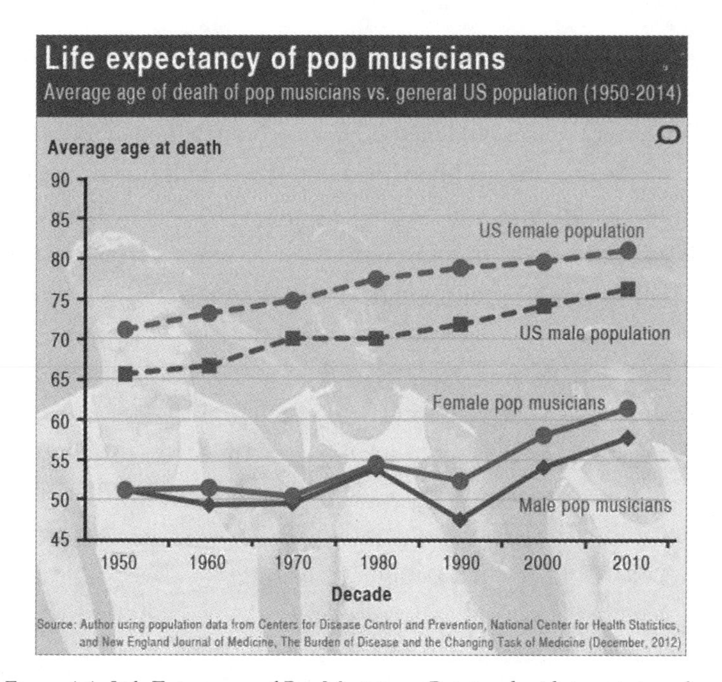

Figure 4.1. Life Expectancy of Pop Musicians. Reprinted with permission of Dr. Dianna Theadora Kenney from her article "Stairway to Hell: Life and Death in the Pop Music Industry," as published in The Conversation.

At the same time, few people choose this lifestyle of the famous or the political without realizing its very public nature and the challenges associated with that public persona. Yet it is this corresponding need to be recognized and critically acclaimed that drives so many toward this ambition. Whether on Broadway or in the movies, the studio or on stage or the ballet theatre, becoming famous has a price—but, for many, a price well worth paying. Living in absolute obscurity, without public recognition or acclaim, is perceived as an even worse destiny.

So too with those choosing a life of politics. Each year, thousands of political figures emerge to be senator, congressperson, governor, county executive, or assemblyman. While the motivations may differ vastly, from true, well-intentioned public service to the cynical means and method to enrich oneself, many political personalities allow no impediments to their ambition or set no boundaries on what will or can be done to achieve it. The term *ruthless politician* may be more accurate than commonly recognized; for politics is not a profession held in high regard, and neither are the politicians who have the power and the glory. In fact, public opinion polls of politicos are nearing bottom. Gallup tracks public opinion on the U.S. House and Senate, and the imagery is generally very negative. Congressional approval descended to a dizzying low rate of 9 percent in 2013 to a slight improvement in 2019 of 18 percent. But the trend re-emerged in 2020–2021 when the rating plunged to 15 percent according to Gallup.[150]

Whether it be in relation to fame, power, or honors, both Aquinas and Aristotle make plain that true happiness will never emerge or arise from these bestowed conditions, for these plaudits and praises are imperfect and temporary by nature and cannot and will not fully satisfy any human agent. All of these states are merely fleeting moments throughout a lifetime, with the bulk of the human activity, day-to-day life, a bit less exhilarating.

Aristotle

Happiness is the realization and perfect exercise of excellence, and this is not conditional, but absolute. And I use the term "conditional" to express that which is

[150] "Congress and the Public," Gallup, accessed January 1, 2022, https://news.gallup.com/poll/1600/congress-public.aspx.

indispensable, and "absolute" to express that which is good in itself.[151]

Aquinas

Consequently, man's happiness cannot consist in fame or glory. On the other hand, man's good depends on God's knowledge as its cause. And therefore man's beatitude depends, as on its cause, on the glory which man has with God.[152]

In this way, it is clear that all fame, honor, and power are transitory states of being, without permanency or perpetuality. As a result, none of these states will ever fully satisfy our natural craving for happiness. Consider this list of "famous" people, all of whom suffered some level of depression or mental sadness:

Anthony Hopkins—actor
Audrey Hepburn—actress
Barbara Bush—former U.S. First Lady
Claude Monet—artist
Cole Porter—musician
Elton John—musician
Ernest Hemingway—writer
Harrison Ford—actor
Jim Carrey—actor/comedian
Joan Rivers—comedian
John Cleese—comedian

[151] *Pol.*, 1331b25-30.
[152] Aquinas, *Summa*, I-II, q. 2, art. 3, corp.

Judy Garland—actress
Laurence Olivier—actor
Marlon Brando—actor
Ozzy Osbourne—musician
Paul Simon—musician
Stephen Hawking—scientist
Yves Saint Laurent—fashion designer[153]

All of them have fame and notoriety; all achieved high-level status in their profession, whether politics, music, the arts or theatre, and science, and all were blessed by extraordinary fortune and benefits, and yet fame, power, and honor could not ward off sadness. In each of these cases, we encounter a state of happiness that has no permanency, nor can it be said to be satisfactory in and of itself. No amount of adulation, at the temporal and human level, will ever deliver the type of happiness that a higher power provides.

The 2014 suicide of the famed and esteemed comedian Robin Williams highlights this earthly incapacity to really be happy in the truest sense of the word. Externally, Robin was a man of many laughs and jocularity, although internally, no matter how much adulation and respect received for his work, there was a void, a vacuum that makes happiness nothing more than a frustrated goal.

Or consider the case of Charlie Sheen, a talented actor from a pedigreed family of actors whose performances in a host of productions evidence a man of many talents. Despite these advantages, Charlie Sheen became consumed by a world of drugs and sexual promiscuity and a general tendency toward a life of vice over virtue.

[153] Simon Worrall, "The Troubled Minds of the Rich and Famous," *National Geographic*, April 9, 2016, accessed May 25, 2019, https://www.nationalgeographic.com/culture/article/160409-famous-people-with-autism-depression-mental-health-psychological-disorders.

Even arrested for his erratic behavior, Charlie Sheen spun out of control, his life a venue without much chance at human happiness either in the temporal or transcendent sense.

Aristotle and Aquinas are fully aware of the transitory nature of fame, power, and glory and, due to this fundamental inadequacy, will look elsewhere for a happiness that has more punch and permanency. Each is acutely aware of the natural limitations that earthly happiness brings, for common sense dictates that the affairs of human beings are no longer in duration than the moment, the hour, and the lifespan.

Aristotle

If then, there is some end of the things we do, which we desire for its own sake (everything else being desired for the sake of this), and if we do not choose everything for the sake of something else (for at that rate the process would go on to infinity, so that our desire would be empty and vain), clearly this must be the good and the chief good.[154]

Aquinas

Now the universe of creatures, to which man is compared as a part to whole, is not the last end, but is ordained to God, as to its last end. Therefore the last end of man is not the good of the universe, but God Himself.[155]

[154] *Nic. Ethics*, 1093a15–25.

[155] Aquinas, *Summa*, I–II, q. 2, art. 8, ad 2.

Fame, Glory, Honor, and the Concept of Happiness

So many people pine and yearn for fame and for a wide variety of motivations. In some cases, the desire for fame becomes almost obsessional—using people and circumstances to achieve that status—caring little for the well-being of those who helped us move up the ladder of success and fame. Others crave fame to bolster insecurity and incompleteness, using the corresponding public adulation to fill in those spots in our psyche or emotional bank with the notoriety that comes from fame. Still others see fame as a sort of personal vindication or actualization by concluding that fame complements talent and ability. Though rarer, some parties see fame as an affirmation of a particular talent or skill, tempered by intelligent judgment and an ambition that is neither vainglorious nor too humble to keep the virtuous mean. In other words, there is nothing wrong with the pursuit of fame if done with virtue and respect for others. Too often the means to fame become the driving and overly ambitious tact to succeed no matter who is hurt along the way or at the expense of what is truly more important in a human life.

Aristotle

> We blame both the ambitious man as aiming at honour more than is right and from wrong sources, and the unambitious man as not willing to be honoured even for noble reasons.... But sometimes we praise the ambitious man as being manly and a lover of what is noble, and the unambitious man as being moderate and temperate.[156]

[156] *Nic. Ethics*, 1125b5–15.

Aquinas

> That man desires honor above all else, arises from his natural desire for happiness, from which honor results.... Wherefore man seeks to be honored especially by the wise, on whose judgment he believes himself to be excellent or happy.[157]

In this way, Aristotle and Aquinas promote the idea of fame, glory, and honor tied to a virtuous disposition. Achieving the moral excellence both thinkers so often espouse comes about for many reasons, one of which is the proper praise and honor given those who live in accordance with virtue. To recognize and laud a person of extraordinary character, or, put another way, to give honor and glory to those acting in accordance with right reason and the virtuous disposition, is not something to be condemned. In fact, moral education demands that we single out and profusely praise and honor those living rightly. Of course, this conclusion does not equate with any idea that fame, honor, and glory will be the recipe for perpetual happiness, for that state is reserved for the transcendent good of which we have often referred. However, any culture striving for moral and behavioral excellence must connect the role of fame, honor, and glory to those who aspire to the highest standards. Such recognition needs to reward those worthy of our acclimation and honor.

On the other hand, Aristotle and Aquinas conclude that the use of fame, glory, and honor as a foundational means for human happiness cannot achieve that state of happiness, for a person's

[157] Aquinas, *Summa*, I–II, q. 2, art. 2, ad 3.

"good depends on God's knowledge" and the "glory which man has with God."[158] Entertainers and famous people often forget the priority of things and become consumed with artificial substitutes for happiness in the form of drugs and alcohol.[159]

And while it is chic to critique the acting and music industry, due to its elevated rate of tragedies when compared to the general population, some performers are quite able to maintain that balance between personal honor and fame, and a virtuous disposition that keeps all of it in the proper context. For example, actor Gary Sinise has been passionate about the care of wounded soldiers and first responders returning from our nation's multiple wars, so much so that he expends not only money and time in this worthy charitable cause but has also sublimated his own career interests because of it. On two fronts he is properly given honor and praise—first, his individual talent as an actor; second, as an extraordinary philanthropist to a worthy endeavor.[160] Even with this remarkable story, neither Gary Sinise nor any other party will ever achieve perfect happiness in these earthly affairs, although it is a safe bet that his foundation activities provide a continuous source of joy and meaning in his own life. And there are other stories like this. The Justin J. Watt Foundation, established by professional football player J. J. Watt, is another remarkable example of

[158] Aquinas, *Summa*, I–II, q. 2, art. 2, corp.

[159] For a comprehensive listing of celebrities and the drugs that contributed to their deaths, read the intriguing article by Chris Elkins, "Which Celebrities Have Battled with Addiction?," DrugRehab.com, May 17, 2018, accessed May 25, 2019, https://www.drugrehab.com/addiction/celebrities.

[160] Visit the Gary Sinise Foundation's website at https://www.garysinisefoundation.org to learn more about the actor and the wonderful endeavors of the foundation.

generosity to schools across the country. Few organizations exhibit more passion for aiding others and advancing the community than this foundation.[161] In the final analysis, the hope and chance for fame, glory, and honor is not always a negative, for famous people do wondrous things every day in our culture. But it is those who see the balance in personal success and care for others that deserve our positive affirmation.

Even in the most positive cases cited above, the human agent can never really achieve complete happiness. Charitable works, though always commendable, are also transitory and ephemeral, and while often commencing with proper motive, they can morph into not-for-profit nightmares. At times, charitable groups and organizations lose their foundational bearings and, while still addressing initial reasons for existence, often play down the charity and engage in too much self-enrichment. Many charities have been accused of having excessive administrative costs and salaries at the expense of the mission. Some not only pay excessive salaries but also employ professional fundraisers that pocket a large portion of the funds donated. Charity Navigator tracks the worst offenders in figure 4.2.[162]

In these instances, the praise and honor is not an appropriate response because of the corrupt purpose or motive in that economic redistribution. From this vantage point, Aristotle and Aquinas deduce that perfect happiness can never be fully experienced in fame, honor, glory, and power. From these examples of bloated administrative overhead, we readily discern that the "truth"

[161] Visit the Justin J. Watt Foundation's website at http://jjwfoundation.org/the-foundation/our-progress.

[162] "Ten Charities Overpaying Their For-Profit Fundraisers," Charity Navigator, accessed January 1, 2022, https://www.charitynavigator.org/index.cfm?bay=topten.detail&listid=28.

10 Charities Overpaying their For-Profit Fundraisers

These 10 charities spend more than 50% of their budgets paying for-profit fundraising professionals to solicit your hard-earned money. They are ranked by the percentage of their total functional expenses spent on professional fundraising fees. As a result, very little of the charity's spending is directed towards its programs and services.

Rank	Charity	Program Expenses	Professional Fundraising Fees
1	Cancer Survivors' Fund	8.5%	88.1%
2	The Committee for Missing Children	7.0%	84.4%
3	Autism Spectrum Disorder Foundation	15.9%	80.1%
4	Childhood Leukemia Foundation	16.2%	79.5%
5	Firefighters Charitable Foundation	9.3%	77.6%
6	Kids Wish Network	14.1%	63.2%
7	HonorBound Foundation	17.7%	54.2%
8	Purple Heart Foundation	23.6%	51.7%
9	Veterans Support Foundation	25.1%	43.4%
10	Find the Children	29.6%	39.2%

Figure 4.2. Charities Overpaying for Fundraisers. Reprinted with permission from Charity Navigator.

or "purpose" of the charity is not the end or goal of charitable giving. This type of discrepancy generates false praise and honor.

Aristotle

But people of superior refinement and of active disposition identify happiness with honor; for this is roughly speaking the end of the political life. But it seems too superficial to be what we are looking for, since it is thought to depend on those who bestow honor rather than on him who receives it, but the good we divine to be something of one's own and not really taken from one.[163]

[163] *Nic. Ethics*, 1095b10–15.

Aquinas

Furthermore, we must observe that human knowledge often fails.... For this reason, human glory is frequently deceptive. But since God cannot be deceived, His glory is always true.[164]

Power and the Concept of Happiness

That power drives humanity in both positive and negative ways can easily be observed in modern-day political antics at the federal and state levels. Studies have shown that the acquisition of power may lead to positive emotions, which include some level of happiness.[165] In contrast, "powerless" people often see the world in more negative terms and as a result find contentment more difficult to achieve.[166] None of these observations are scientifically perfect, but a wide array of studies confirm this difference.[167]

What a person will do to maintain power is quite telling. Politicians that are beyond the age of normal retirement cling to their positions without regard for their own competency or effectiveness, for in the world of indifference, what matters is the maintenance

[164] Aquinas, *Summa*, I–II, q. 2, art. 3, corpus.

[165] J. D. Datu, "Why Power Does Not Guarantee Happiness across Cultures," *Online Readings in Psychology and Culture* 5, no. 3 (2014): 4.

[166] Ibid., 5.

[167] Ana Guinote, "Power and Goal Pursuit," *Personality and Social Psychology Bulletin* 33, no. 8 (2007): 1076–1087, accessed May 25, 2019, http://dx.doi.org/10.1177/0146167207301011; Joris Lammers et al., "Power Gets the Job: Priming Power Improves Interview Outcomes," *Journal of Experimental Social Psychology* 49, no. 4 (2013): 776–779, accessed May 25, 2019, http://dx.doi.org/10.1016/j.jesp.2013.02.008.

of power over all else. This type of claim has been made against the current speaker of the U.S. House of Representatives, Nancy Pelosi. Her own Democratic Party showed resistance to her continuing appointment to this rule for a host of reasons, including an inability to work with the opposition, an intransigent mentality on many topics in need of cooperation and joint venture, an ideological mentality that makes legislative compromise difficult, and her age now exceeding eighty. Sixteen new congresspersons voted for alternative leadership. The same critique could be made of the current president, Joseph Biden, whose age and related health concerns, not unsurprisingly so as he approaches eighty, are becoming more scrutinized. And is power so narcotic that it must be maintained despite age and infirmity? While no one denies an accomplished life in so many contexts, there is a balance that need be achieved in matters of power, especially knowing when to pass on the gavel to a new generation of leadership. Unfortunately, Nancy Pelosi is not alone, as the House and the Senate are filled with people that have held power for far too long, which in turn leads to entrenched positioning and an ineffectual governance process (see figure 4.3).

It is quite obvious that when parties cling frantically to their positions of authority and power, it's as if the loss of these slots would remove all meaning from life. And in a sense, it is power that corrupts both the person and the collective that suffers under it, absolutely. Certainly, no one suggests that having a purpose in life through the continuance in an occupation or profession is a bad thing. However, the obsessive, twenty-four-hour-a-day lust for power, so evident, so manifest in our political class, will never bring happiness and contentment. Because power depends on something or someone else, it is not self-sufficient or perfect by design; it is not universal or absolute and it is not something unchangeable. Indeed, the very opposite is true and thus, as a result, power can never deliver

Figure 4.3. The Honorable Speaker of the House, Nancy Pelosi.

the sort of happiness that provides perpetual comfort. Power lies not exclusively in the political realm but in positions of corporate and business oversight, religious orders and church hierarchical structures, and any locus where decision-making over others resides.

Power may or may not be legitimately earned or justified, so in this sense, we can never depend on power as the measure for happiness. Tyrants, dictators, and totalitarian leaders all possessed extraordinary levels of power, although none of that strength and control seems to have translated into human happiness. Surely, Adolf Hitler's final days in the Berlin bunker, under siege from every corner of his country, were not happy, nor for that matter is it questionable, regardless of his power, whether he was ever very happy. See figure 4.4.[168]

[168] "The Last Picture of Adolf Hitler, 1945," Rare Historical Photos, accessed May 25, 2019, https://rarehistoricalphotos.com/last-picture-adolf-hitler-1945.

Figure 4.4. Last Picture of Adolf Hitler in the Crumbling Reichstag, April 28, 1945.

Aristotle

For there is required . . . not only complete excellence but also a complete life, since many changes occur in life, and all manner of chances, and the most prosperous may fall into great misfortunes in old age.[169]

Aquinas

Happiness is the most perfect good. But power is the most imperfect.[170]

[169] *Nic. Ethics*, 1100a1–5.

[170] Aquinas, *Summa*, I–II, q. 2, art. 4, sc.

Power, like fame, glory, and honor, is an external condition to the question of human happiness. Power is attained and then lost, modified then relegated or delegated, grows and diminishes. Power lacks the permanency and universality to be the driving engine for happiness. While both Aristotle and Aquinas admit that power can be a productive and very beneficial exercise, its lack of self-sufficiency and dependability causes it to fail in the question of pure, unadulterated happiness. The "good use of power"[171] can and does lead to a parcel of the happiness state, but that composed moment cannot encompass an eternal lifetime. As with fame, honor, and glory, power can be utilized for all the wrong purposes, and in this sense, power is about "good and evil."[172]

Given this chameleon-like quality, power can never serve as the rock-hard, foundational purpose for human happiness. Like fame and wealth, its attractiveness compels people to the far edges of conduct in order to preserve power. Joseph Stalin killed and executed thousands of his enemies—a class of people that he termed or perceived as adversaries after his ascent to power. See figure 4.5.

So ruthless and satanic was Joseph Stalin that he orchestrated the death of scores of human beings, from purposeful executions in the millions, to direct, intentional starvation of whole groups of people as in Ukraine, to a highly developed system of Gulags—prisons for political enemies and undesirables. By some estimates, his clutch on power generated nearly sixty million deaths. From the Communist Civil War at the turn of the twentieth century to the post-Stalin era of the 1960s, the numbers of deaths are almost

[171] Aquinas, *Summa*, I–II, q. 2, art. 4, ad 2.
[172] Aquinas, *Summa*, I–II, q. 2, art. 4, corp.

Figure 4.5. Joseph Stalin: Ruler of the Soviet World.

incalculable because Stalin wanted his power preserved at all or any costs.[173]

Stalin, Hitler, and others like Mao all illustrate how power can be utilized for the most sinister reasons and dastardly rationales. And in each generation leaders and dictators reach new levels of evil, ruthlessly punishing the very people they are responsible for. Afghanistan's Taliban are the perfect picture of ruthlessness, and the outlook, given our horrid pullout from the country, is bleak. Syria has descended into an almost catastrophic state because its leader refuses to treat his people with virtue and justice and just as tenaciously clutches at power he no longer has the moral authority to hold. With nearly five hundred thousand of his countrymen dead over the last decade, parts of

[173] Review the astounding statistics at R. J. Rummel, "Deka-Megamurderers," accessed May 25, 2019, https://hawaii.edu/powerkills/MEGA.HTM.

the country reduced to complete rubble, and human suffering now normative in Syria, is power ever worth this cost? Or could Putin's genocidal campaign in the Ukraine ever be justified or rationalized as acceptable human behavior? Power drives the actor to extreme injustice and the type of war crimes that are never defensible.

Power may emanate from a zealous, theocratic, and very radical ideology that offends the sensibilities of ordinary people, such as in the case of ISIS—the Islamic radical group that declared a caliphate against its Muslim neighbors and then proceeded to take over large swathes of land in the Middle East while terrorizing the general population, especially reserving its animus for those who did not adopt the extreme, more fundamentalist form of Islam. Some of their more insidious practices include:

- Murdering innocents
- Persecuting Christians, Yazidis, and other religious minorities
- Forced conversions
- Torture and mutilation
- Oppression of women
- Slavery
- Concubinage
- Harsh punishments
- Jihad
- Declaring a global Islamic state (caliphate)

ISIS abuses have been met with universal condemnation and extraordinary sacrifices by soldiers and sailors from a host of countries—a reality that can never be forgotten, since power without check or moral foundation gravely injures individuals and communities. The United States, the Kurds of Northern Iraq, and other NATO countries have made extraordinary sacrifices to crush

Figure 4.6. Department of Defense: U.S. Howitzer Attacks on ISIS Positions.

the caliphate from its once extended territory to fundamental annihilation as announced in early 2019. See figure 4.6.[174]

Power grows and subsides in the evilest of regimes, and in fact, as Aristotle and Aquinas both declare, such tyrannies cannot last long. A quick look at the map that illustrates the shrinkage of ISIS power during the period of 2015–2019 is quite telling.

All of these examples of leaders exerting power and control display the temporality of power and why power alone cannot be a source of real happiness. Power cannot avoid natural change, the ebb and flow of who controls and who does not; power never rests in any absolute setting but in changeable events and circumstances.

[174] Terri Moon Cronk, "DOD Spokesman: ISIS Deliberately Misuses Mosques," U.S. Department of Defense, October 23, 2018, accessed May 25, 2019, https://www.defense.gov/explore/story/Article/1669289/dod-spokesman-isisdeliberately-misuses-mosques.

The power of Hitler's thousand-year Reich lasted less than twenty-two years while ISIS crumbled in six. Even well-disposed, just societies, driven by better motives, cannot last forever, as the Romans and Greeks make plain. Power, like fame, is fleeting and not a foundational bedrock for human happiness.

Aristotle

Tyranny is just that arbitrary power of an individual which is responsible to no one ... with a view to its own advantage, not to that of its subjects, and therefore against their will. No freeman willingly endures such a government.[175]

Aquinas

It is impossible for happiness to consist in power.[176]

Conclusion

A persistent inquiry in all civilizations has been whether fame, honors, glory, and power lead to happiness. What appears unarguable is the extent to which human beings will go to get fame and glory as well as honors and power. Much of this chapter has recurrently indicated that happiness cannot exclusively rest or reside in power, fame, and glory alone, and for very good reasons. First, no one can dispute the attractiveness of these states in some normative or virtuous sense. It is far better to be honored for one's

[175] *Pol.*, 1295b20–25.

[176] Aquinas, *Summa*, I–II, q. 2, art. 4, corp.

contribution than to live in complete obscurity without recognition for what a person is due.

Second, a person can lead in power, and do so virtuously. While virtuous leaders are rare birds, history has shown leaders who display a virtuous disposition and inclination to be better angels than the demons often encountered throughout recorded history. Certainly, one could reasonably judge that Winston Churchill acted as a vastly better leader than Joseph Stalin, or that President Harry Truman operated with a bit more goodness than Richard Nixon. Granted all leaders have deficits due to our human nature, and this very condition of imperfection is why power or fame or honors can never truly bring a perfect happiness. Only God, our Creator, who lacks nothing, can deliver that sort of perfection to creatures made in His image. Throughout this discussion, we encounter Aristotle and Aquinas continuously reminding us that these temporal states—of fame, honor, glory, and power—are incapable of generating the happiness we truly seek.

Third, there is a trick here regarding fame, honor, and power, and that deals with how to carry these states for the betterment of self and others. While so many entertainers, athletes, and political figures may start out with the best intentions, too many fall off the tracks in the progression of their careers. To reiterate, there is nothing wrong with using the desire to excel and succeed as the motivator and incentive to be the best one can be. However, too many people cross over into another dimension when laden with such adulation, with such power and such fame, and they begin to believe the hyperbolic descriptions of their own talents or think themselves immune to the ravages of hard lifestyles in drugs and drink. Even more tellingly, they think the rules of virtue and good life do not apply to their conditions. To illustrate, think of Amy

Figure 4.7. Amy Winehouse Singing at the Virgin Festival, Pimlico, Baltimore, Maryland, on August 4, 2007.

Winehouse, a singer of exceptional ability whose trajectory upon achieving success, fame, and honor was nothing but downward. See figure 4.7.[177]

In a sort of immolation of drugs and alcohol, the fame, the glory, and the honors consumed her. The *Daily Mail* chronicled her last hours:

[177] Greg Gebhardt, photo of Amy Winehouse, accessed May 25, 2019, https://commons.wikimedia.org/wiki/File:Amy_Winehouse_-Virgin_ Festival,_ Pimlico,_ Baltimore,_Maryland-4August2007_(cropped).jpg. This file is licensed under the Creative Commons Attribution 2.0 generic license, https://creativecommons.org/licenses/by/2.0.

> Amy Winehouse spent her final hours drinking vodka alone in her bedroom and watching YouTube videos of herself, a court was told yesterday.
>
> A second inquest confirmed the 27-year-old died of alcohol poisoning at her north London home on July 23, 2011.
>
> Miss Winehouse drank so much that she stopped breathing and fell into a coma.
>
> The inquest was re-heard because the coroner at the first hearing did not have the correct qualifications.
>
> St. Pancras Coroners Court was told that the Grammy award-winning singer, who was battling alcoholism and bulimia, spent the night before her death watching clips of herself on her laptop.
>
> She was found dead on her bed 12 hours later, with the laptop beside her and two empty vodka bottles on the floor.[178]

Beyond the disheartening and devastating loss of a young and talented human being, the commentary on her last hours says much about her abject lack of happiness. Despite her public acclaim and honor, regardless of her fame and notoriety, none of these states and conditions could deliver the happiness once thought natural to fame and glory. The last hours of her life, spent in isolation, in a drunken stupor, watching YouTube videos of herself as if caught in a web of unceasing narcissism, manifest the happiness deficit. So intense was this emptiness, this lack of peace and contentment,

[178] Louise Eccles, "Singer Amy Winehouse Died Watching YouTube Videos of Herself after Vodka Binge, Inquest Hears," *Daily Mail*, January 8, 2013, accessed May 25, 2019, https://www.dailymail.co.uk/news/article-2258983/Amy-Winehouse-diedwatching-YouTube-videos-vodka-binge.html.

that all that surrounded her on the day of her death were bottles of vodka and a running loop of self-imagery.

Finally, by no means is this a personal critique of Amy Winehouse, for she is not alone in this distressed state. The world has witnessed too many that fall into the abyss all the while believing that the very fame, glory, and honor craved would somehow fill in the gaps and make a person happy. Neither Amy Winehouse nor Joseph Stalin were happy people, and it is quite apparent that fame failed her and power let Stalin down. Ultimately, each of these states we seek is external from the essential and perfect happiness; each of these states will vary and even completely disappear depending on circumstances, and each of these states will at best be just a sliver of what real happiness means in the transcendent sense. Aristotle and Aquinas constantly remind us of this reality: that our own imperfection and inadequacy will never provide a permanent and perfect happiness and that to avoid going on "ad infinitum" as Aristotle comments, we shall have to find something that lacks nothing, that needs nothing and pines for nothing. Since all of what we experience here on earth is subject to change and alteration, happiness will only be partial and temporary in human operations. Only when God is encountered will happiness have real and perennial meaning.

Rules for a Happy Life

4.0: That Happiness Does Not Arise from Fame and Notoriety

4.1: That Happiness, Which Seeks the Ultimate End, Is Often Diverted by Fame

4.2: That Happiness Is Eternal and Perpetual in God, While Fame Is Fleeting

4.3: That Happiness Is about Others While Fame Is about Self

4.4: That Happiness Equates with Contentment While Fame Craves Status and More
4.5: That Happiness Keeps Proper Priorities While Fame Manifests Inordinate Attention
4.6: That Happiness and Fame Can Be Compatible If Engaged in Charitable Acts
4.7: That Happiness and Fame Are Balanced by the Virtuous Life
4.8: That Happiness and the Lust or Obsession for Power Are Incompatible
4.9: That Happiness and Power, If Used Justly, Can Complement One Another
4.10: That Happiness and Power Are Balanced by the Virtuous Life
4.11: That Happiness Is Undermined When Human Power Is All That Matters
4.12: That Happiness Is Impossible When Power Lacks God—the Ultimate End
4.13: That Happiness Cannot Exist in Power or Glory Alone Due to Its Temporary Condition

5

Is Happiness Derived from the Body and Pleasure?

Introduction

The question of pleasure, especially in the bodily sense, has long been examined in the matter of happiness. It is easy to understand this tendency because pleasure is not by nature inherently wrong, nor is pleasure something to be avoided in all contexts. This is true of all sensual delights, especially in matters involving sexuality, since the propagation of the human species depends on the sexual drive and act. However, the question of pleasure and the body entails so much more than sexuality and includes, but is not limited to, food and drink, as with gluttony, bulimia, the use of alcohol, and the current crisis in drug usage and its many addictive qualities that enslave the body.

In general, a virtuous person knows how to regulate and properly control these actions, seeking not only that ultimate end but also the moderate mean in things—never shunning all pleasure nor devouring it without limitation. So, being virtuous means being an actor who engages sexuality within designated parameters, such as love and marriage, or eats what one needs to thrive and survive but does not gorge and deprive oneself to the point of illness and obsession. Aquinas holds that "some pleasures are good, and that some are evil."[179] However, a narrow and singular pursuit of pleasure is destined not to produce happiness for the human actor. "Pleasures are gifts to be enjoyed, not goals to be pursued."[180]

In the proper context and setting, pleasure comports with and advances some aspects of human happiness, culminating in our ultimate end—our true purpose for human life, that is, to encounter and be with the God who created us. Indeed, Aquinas argues that being in God's presence will be a form of unbridled pleasure. "Accordingly, man's last end may be said to be either God Who is the Supreme Good simply; or the enjoyment of God; which implies a certain pleasure in the last end."[181] Pleasure, however, can be the great deceiver when it becomes the primary end of human conduct. The great Roman lawyer and philosopher, Cicero, referred to it as the "greatest imitator" of truth and goodness.[182]

At its core, pleasure can be derived in many settings, mostly being sensory, whether by touch or smell, taste or palate, ear or eyes—we encounter pleasurable things each and every day. In modern life, literally every boundary once taken for granted has been thrown on the ash heap of moral relativity. So promiscuous sexual activity, filled with sensory pleasure, is not to be constrained, or gluttonous food obsession, or the inordinate cravings of being high or drunk—all of these sensory experiences have no current limitations. Aristotle refers to a person who cannot check or properly

[179] Aquinas, *Summa*, I-II, q. 34, art. 1, corp.

[180] Eugene Peterson, "The Pursuit of Happiness Is a Dead-End Street," *Christianity Today* 61, no. 5 (June 2017): 71–74.

[181] Aquinas, *Summa*, I-II, q. 34, art. 1, corp.

[182] Marcus Tullius Cicero, *On the Laws*, trans. David Fott (Ithaca, NY: Cornell University Press, 2014), I.34.

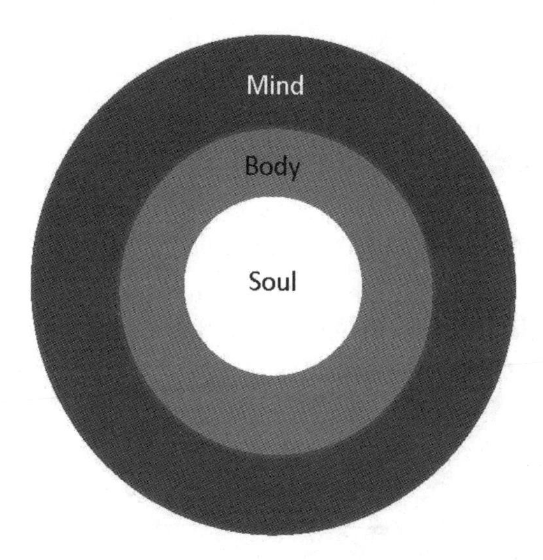

Figure 5.1. Relationship of Mind, Body, and Soul.

measure his sensory slavishness as "incontinent."[183] From another angle, we encounter hosts of individuals who are obsessed with the state of their bodies—endlessly working out, measuring and gauging the fat content, the skin condition, or the elimination of aging. The body—the senses, the pleasure natural to those senses—has taken a preeminent position over other priorities long held in Western thought. The traditional priority of our parts, so to speak—the spirit, the mind, and the body—has been largely upended or inverted in the modern world, to the point that one's spirit has been reduced to superstition and the intellect, the mind deemed less important than the body itself (see figure 5.1).

Our culture's current obsession with plastic surgery, the avoidance of aging, and the cookie-cutter bodily imagery says much about

[183] *Nic. Ethics*, 1150a.

our changing priorities. On the other hand, happiness can and does depend upon a healthy and well-cared-for body. The human suffering from physical illness or poor care does have its price. Even so, that price is dwarfed against the most crucial components of the human person, the soul and the mind or reason.

Since the human body cannot avoid, as Aristotle would put it, its own corruption over time, it cannot be the central basis for happiness, because the body ends. No matter how many face reconstructions, tummy tucks, implants, or pectoral uplifts occur, the body cannot outlast the ravages of time. For this reason alone, the body, in and of itself, cannot bring true happiness that lasts.

Aristotle

Now, since some pleasures are necessary while others are not, and are necessary up to a point while the excesses of them are not, nor are the deficiencies, and this is equally true of appetites and pains, the man who pursues the excesses of things pleasant, or pursues to excess necessary objects . . . is self-indulgent, for such a man is of necessity without regrets, and therefore incurable, since a man without regrets cannot be cured.[184]

Aquinas

Because bodily delights are generally known, the name of pleasure has been appropriated to them (*Ethic.* Viii, 13) although other delights excel them; and yet happiness

[184] *Nic. Ethics*, 1150a15–22.

> does not consist in them. . . . But bodily pleasure cannot result from the perfect good even in that way.[185]

The challenges for achieving happiness are many and varied, and our sensory experiences relating to the body often deceive or mislead us in our journey to that state of peace and contentment. As already noted, the issue here is largely a question of balance—reconciling the natural pleasure that emanates or emerges from selected bodily activity while at the same time assuring that what we enjoy or encounter in the bodily sphere is consistent with a virtuous disposition and a life well lived. Pleasure can become an "idol" in one's life, for "what he ought to control now controls him."[186] This can be a challenge for the body, and pleasure in a sensory sense deceives us in the matter of actual goodness and proper ends for the human life, or as Aristotle puts it, "it is no easy task to be good."[187]

All of us encounter the challenges in the smallest to the most complex problems in day-to-day operations. To illustrate, the balance between too many potato chips, too many chocolate-covered peanuts or cherries, or just the right amount cannot ever be reduced to a perfect equation. It would be folly to argue that lines get crossed in matters of food, of sensuality, of beauty and attractiveness, of feelings and satisfaction. It is the same lack of reason that drives unexpected pregnancy, resulting in nonmarital situations by the abandonment of moral boundaries we hope to maintain but fail to honor, or allowing an admirable gaze toward a beautiful

[185] Aquinas, *Summa*, I–II, q. 2, art. 6, corp.
[186] Peterson, "Happiness," 72.
[187] *Nic. Ethics*, 1109a20–25.

woman or handsome man to descend from admiration to a lust. None of this is posed to justify or permit things but instead to exemplify how complex the matter of the body and its corresponding pleasure can be. See table 5.1.

Love	Lust
Gives	Takes
Waits	Impatient
Respects	Violates
Forgives	Condemns
Unselfish	Selfish
Generous	Greedy
Protects	Harmful
Faithful	Disloyal
Upholds	Abandons

Table 5.1. Love versus Lust.

Love in its purest form, perfect, unconditional love, produces a vastly different state of mind and passion than the party driven by lust. For most people, that tension challenges the development of meaningful relationships, and most commentators see how in short supply those relationships have become in our appearance-driven society.

Aristotle

But we must consider the things toward which we ourselves also are easily carried away.... And this will be recognizable from the pleasure and the pain we feel. We must drag ourselves away to the contrary extreme, for we shall get into the intermediate state by drawing well away from error, as people do in straightening sticks that are bent.[188]

Aquinas

Consequently it is evident that good which is fitting for the body, and which caused delight through being apprehended by sense, is not man's perfect good, is quite a trifle as compared with the good of the soul.... And therefore, bodily pleasure is neither happiness itself, nor a proper accident of happiness.[189]

What follows is a series of examples and edifications of these general conclusions regarding the prioritization of the spirit and the soul over the body and sensory experience—an idea consistent with both Plato and Aristotle, who argued that "contemplation and the contemplative life" provide the best chance for happiness,[190] and with Aquinas, who continually reiterates the supremacy of our ultimate end in God.

The Incapacity of the Body and Sensory Pleasure in the Pursuit of Happiness

One of the most striking faults in modern logic about how to live a good and happy life is the conclusion that how one's body feels actually has a pressing connection to the question of human

[188] *Nic. Ethics*, 1109a1–6.

[189] Aquinas, *Summa*, I–II, q. 2, art. 6, corp.

[190] *Nic. Ethics*, 1095a–b.

happiness. When speaking of the feel of the body, we are not dealing with health and illness, for happiness does properly connect to the state of our overall health and the challenges of sickness. A healthy person, unchallenged by serious illness or disease, has a better chance at contentment than one suffering from chronic disease or ongoing illness. Instead, this incapacity of the body and sensory pleasure deals with other matters, such as the exclusive view that being "fit" or at "perfect weight" or in possession of an idyllic body mass index[191] leads to human happiness. To be sure, such achievements are very worthy goals and something to be commended, although it is very unlikely that these conditions alone would ever lead to a perfect and unassailable form of happiness.

One might also consider that happiness will result from multiple sexual relations with multiple parties—setting a sort of perverse conquering goal that proves attractiveness or sexual prowess—an erroneous belief that too will falter in time. In fact, most studies now confirm that a sexual lifestyle, once termed promiscuous, brings forth a host of problems that thwart rather than advance human happiness. And the more remote the sexual relation, labeled autonomous or nonautonomous, the worse the depression becomes.[192]

On the issue of happiness alone, the party engaging with diverse and myriad sexual partners is far more likely to encounter a range of social, moral, and legal problems, from children born out of wedlock, multiple abortions, and increased substance abuse,

[191] "About Adult BMI," Centers for Disease Control and Prevention, June 3, 2022, https://www.cdc.gov/healthyweight/assessing/bmi/adult_bmi/index.html.

[192] See Bersamin et al., "Risky Business: Is There an Association between Casual Sex and Mental Health among Emerging Adults?," *Journal of Sex Research* 51, no. 1 (2014): 43–51.

thereby being unhappier than the party that remains prudent and temperate in sexual activity.[193] The Heritage Foundation charts Centers for Disease Control and Prevention (CDC) data outlining the great benefit of delaying sexual activity by demonstrating its correlation to human happiness itself. See figure 5.2.[194]

Another study conducted by the U.S. Department of Health and Human Services in 2020 essentially confirms a host of benefits for the younger generation from delayed sexual activity. See figure 5.3.[195]

From another perspective, it is popular to argue that prostitution's ill effects are largely a convention invented by moralists and do-gooders. In modern circles, selling sexual activity for money, the body and its flesh for economic reward, has become either a form of economic empowerment or a private act outside the realm of any judgment and, in the final analysis, does not impact the happiness quotient for the average human person. Most studies of prostitutes paint a very different picture.

In prostitution, happiness is replaced with depression, anxiety, substance abuse and addiction, de-sensitivity to normal human interaction, and general assault on the integrity and sanctity of the human person. A recent study of Swiss prostitution workers

[193] See Robert E. Rector et al., *The Harmful Effects of Early Sexual Activity and Multiple Sexual Partners among Women: A Book of Charts*, Heritage Foundation (June 3, 2003).

[194] Ibid., 13.

[195] Dana Rotz et al., *Assessing the Benefits of Delayed Sexual Activity: A Synthesis of the Literature*, OPRE Report #2020-04 (Washington, DC: Office of Planning, Research, and Evaluation, Administration for Children and Families, U.S. Department of Health and Human Services, 2020), 3, accessed January 1, 2022, at https://www.acf.hhs.gov/sites/default/files/documents/opre/benefitsofsexdelay_litreview_508_final_0.pdf

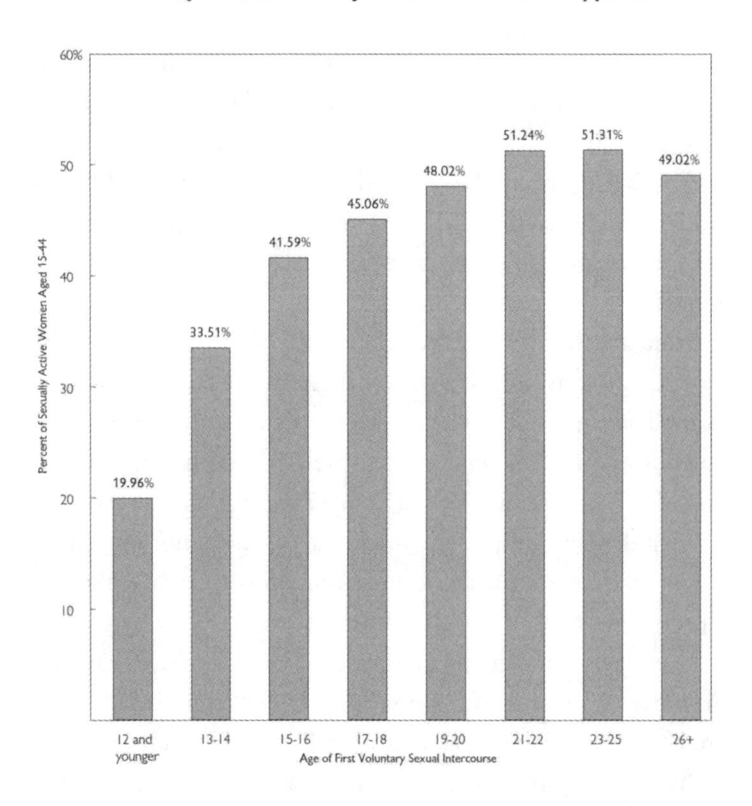

Figure 5.2. Sexual Activity Delay versus Happiness. Source: CDC, National Center for Health Statistics, National Survey of Family Growth, 1995.

shows explicitly how the body's abuse for prostitution purposes leads to significantly higher levels of distress than its contrary.[196]

[196] W. Rössler et al., "The Mental Health of Female Sex Workers," *Acta Psychiatrica Scandinavica* 122, no. 2 (2010): 7, accessed May 27, 2019, https://www.collegium.ethz.ch/fileadmin/autoren/pdf_papers/10_roessler_sexwork.pdf.

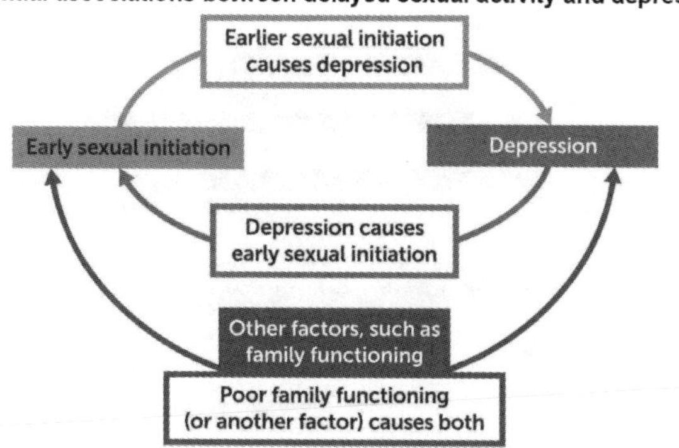

Figure 5.3. Potential Associations between Delayed Sexual Activity and Depression.

Just as destined for a dead-end street will be the endless efforts to stay young, to not age, or to not show the signs of aging by medical intervention of every sort. The range of services and associated fees with this effort to maintain youthful appearances are charted by the American Society of Plastic Surgeons, a list that delineates the unbounded efforts to achieve a temporary and very superficial form of happiness. See figure 5.4.[197]

The body's capacity to generate happiness or, to put it in contemporary parlance, to "feel good about one's self-image" will ultimately fail because the body cannot be our ultimate end or purpose. In modern culture, the body has been elevated to levels that in most of Western tradition would be almost inconceivable. Happiness cannot be rooted in corporeal matter, because it has a limited lifespan,

[197] American Society of Plastic Surgeons, *Plastic Surgery Statistics Report* (2021), accessed January 1, 2022, https://www.plasticsurgery.org/documents/News/Statistics/2020/plastic-surgery-statistics-full-report-2020.pdf.

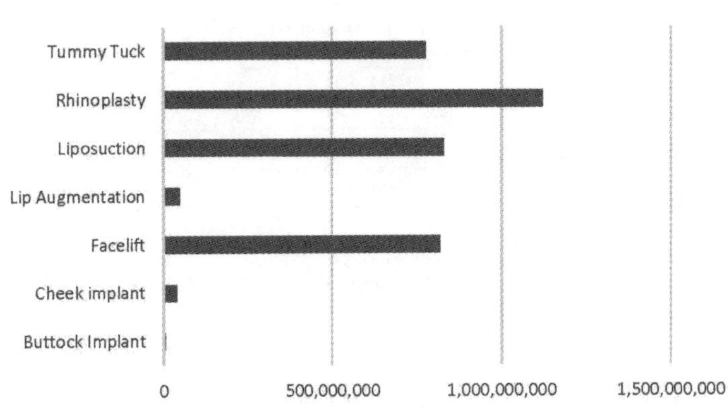

Figure 5.4. Plastic Surgeon Expenditures.

or as St. Thomas More told Cromwell in Robert Bolt's *A Man for All Seasons*, "Death comes for us all. Even for Kings he comes."[198]

There are a bevy of other reasons the body will not generate true happiness. First, the body moves rather than contemplates, for in happiness the human agent must comprehend the perfect good or the ultimate end of a human life. No "body" has that capacity, for each part of the body functions without any form of rationality or thought. For the body at best seeks to preserve itself as well as it can, to sustain and nurture, to grow and flourish rather than seek its own destruction. But this type of care and feeding is over a lifespan, not eternity, and true happiness finds a home only in the eternal realm. The body cannot be a human person's last end, nor be the means to happiness tied to the "preservation of its own being."[199] Second, since the body and soul are the matter and form

[198] See the excerpts from the script of *A Man for All Seasons* at http://www.sjsu.edu/faculty/wooda/149F/week-4-seasons-script.pdf.

[199] Aquinas, *Summa*, I–II, q. 2, art. 6, corp.

of the human being, the higher power of the soul can exist without a body, but a body cannot survive without a soul. By contrast, the soul is immortal while the body deteriorates. Hence, the body can never lead to our ultimate happiness because of its limited existence.

Aristotle

But clearly, the excellence we must study is human excellence, for the good we were seeking was human good and human happiness. By human excellence we mean not that of the body but that of the soul and happiness we call an activity of the soul.[200]

Now the mass of mankind are evidently quite slavish in their tastes, preferring a life suitable to the beasts.[201]

Aquinas

Wherefore all the good of the body are ordained to the goods of the soul, as to their end. Consequently, happiness, which is man's last end, cannot consist in goods of the body.[202]

Now good pertaining to the body, and apprehended by sense, cannot be man's perfect good.[203]

The body serves during a limited lifespan and, as a result, can never be the measure of perpetual human happiness. And given this ephemeral nature, decisions regarding the right way to live

[200] *Nic. Ethics*, 1102a10–17.

[201] *Nic. Ethics*, 1095b15–20.

[202] Aquinas, *Summa*, I–II, q. 2, art. 6, corp.

[203] Ibid.

and how to live should never be rationalized by the body alone. In contemporary arguments, the body is often touted as the justification for a position, examples being how the body feels right as to transgendered, homosexual, or other modified sexual status. The listing LGBTQIP++ gets longer by the day, and most of the debate centers on the body rather than the soul or other metaphysical measures. Longitudinal studies are now demonstrating how these sexual identity demands, often driven by the pressures exerted by the body, are matters generating long-term regret and wishes for a reversal in that decision.[204] Data also demonstrate that suicide rates, as well as levels of mental disorder, are higher in the LGBTQ community than in the general population.[205] One study concluded that a longitudinal study on sex reassignment manifests a sample that persons "with transsexualism, after sex reassignment, have considerably higher risks for mortality, suicidal behaviour, and psychiatric morbidity than the general population."[206] Even with all of this, the upward trek of those seeking or identifying with gender reassignment protocols continues.[207] Using the body as

[204] See Stig-Eric Olsson and Anders Möller, "Regret after Sex Reassignment Surgery in a Male-to-Female Transsexual: A Long-Term Follow-Up," *Archives of Sexual Behavior* 35, no. 4 (2006): 501–506, accessed May 27, 2019, https://link.springer.com/article/10.1007%2Fs10508-006-9040-8.

[205] See Cecilia Dhejne et al., "Long-Term Follow-Up of Transsexual Persons Undergoing Sex Reassignment Surgery: Cohort Study in Sweden," *PLoS ONE* 6, no. 2 (2011): e16885, accessed May 27, 2019, https://journals.plos.org/plosone/article?id=10.1371/journal.pone.0016885.

[206] Ibid.

[207] Anna Brown, "5 Key Findings about LGBT Americans," Pew Research Center, June 13, 2017, accessed May 27, 2019, http://pewrsr.ch/2rekSpA.

a moral determinant will likely lead to bad moral reasoning, at least in most cases. Certainly, it is doubtful happiness shall ever be drawn from the body itself due to its corruptibility.

Aquinas lays out a third rationale for why the body is never a bona fide foundation for true happiness—its own inadequacy when compared to other creatures in the natural world. Thomas rightly concludes that other mammals, without reason and rationality, have bodies that move more quickly, that can withstand various attacks on the body with greater effectiveness and can survive physical challenges more capably than any human actor can. Thomas states in part, "Man surpasses all other animals in regard to happiness. But in bodily goods he is surpassed by many animals; for instance, by the elephant for longevity, by the lion in strength, by the stag in fleetness. Therefore man's happiness does not consist in the goods of the body."[208]

If the lion or tiger cannot be acquirers of true happiness, and yet their bodily characteristics can surpass the physical attributes of nearly all men and women, then the body can never be the measure and means to true happiness. In fact, the body causes a host of issues directly in opposition to happiness, such as but not limited to:

- Self-image problems: bulimia and anorexia
- Self-image problems: self-mutilation and excess tattooing
- Carnal lust: inordinate affection or perversity of affections toward the body or its parts
- Disproportionate time and attention given the body at the expense of the soul or spirit
- Judging others based on the appearance of the body
- Body shaming

[208] Aquinas, *Summa*, I–II, q. 2, art. 5, sc.

- Obsession with weight and appearance
- Evaluation of character and person based on the condition of the body[209]

In the quest for happiness, the body provides only limited and narrow opportunities for joy and contentment, especially when compared to the human soul.

Lastly, the incapacity of the human body to deliver true happiness is further proven by its remoteness from happiness itself. Aside from the body's inferiority to the soul, its dependence on the soul for its form, and its own eventual corruption and death, the pleasures that arise from the body lack any permanent or eternal state either. The sensory experiences, the appetitive reactions, the passions that emerge from sexual intensity by way of example do not last, for these experiences cannot remain eternally. Bodily pleasure, in a way, is very, very remote from the idea and essence of pure happiness. Those sensory delights, those fulfilled desires are temporary events depending on much more than the body itself.

Happiness, the Body, and Sexuality

Aristotle

> Choice does not belong to the brutes while sensual desire and anger are common to men and the brutes. The incontinent man acts in conformity with sensual desire.[210]

[209] See "Statistics and Research on Eating Disorders," NEDA, accessed May 27, 2019, https://www.nationaleatingdisorders.org/statistics-research-eating-disorders.

[210] *Nic. Ethics*, 1111b10–15.

Aquinas

All things seek pleasure in the same way as they seek good.... But, just as it happens that not every good which is desired, is of itself and verily good; so not every pleasure is of itself and verily good.[211]

The temperate man does not shun all pleasures, but those that are immoderate, and contrary to reason.[212]

If contemporary media were a reliable barometer of happiness, then sexuality would be a universal path to happiness. Displayed in the most cavalier and abbreviated way, and with dizzying arrays of partners and activities, the sexual mantra has long been equated with a door or path to human happiness. And in this sense, it is all about the body and how particular activities associated with sexual movement give the world boundless glee and sensory exhilaration. If the body is incapable of delivering any meaningful or permanent happiness, its secondary actions, whatever they may be, are even more impossibly tied to the prospect. One does not get happy, in the truest sense of the word, because of sexual agency. One may experience sensory pleasure for the time or the moment, but taken alone, in its individual clinical sense, sexual activity cannot deliver authentic happiness. The "sexual revolution" of the late 1960s into the present has sold a defective bill of goods in more ways than one. Syphilis, chlamydia, and gonorrhea, the three main forms of STDs, are rising at alarming rates, according to the CDC. See figure 5.5.[213]

[211] Aquinas, *Summa*, I–I, q. 34, art. 2, ad 3.

[212] Aquinas, *Summa*, I–II, q. 34, art. 1, ad 2.

[213] Centers for Disease Control and Prevention, *Sexually Transmitted Disease Surveillance 2019* (Atlanta: U.S. Department of Health and

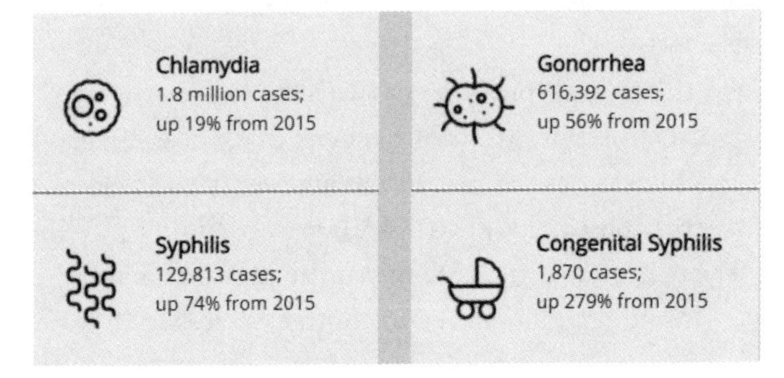

Figure 5.5. Reported STDs in the United States Reach All-Time High for Sixth Consecutive Year. More than 2.5 Million Cases of Chlamydia, Gonorrhea, and Syphilis Were Reported in 2019.

There are many ironies in this setting, although none is more compelling than the promise of happiness and the eventual pathologies that arise and emerge from unrestrained sexual activity. It is the contrary that holds true—that a moderate and bordered sexual lifestyle, grounded in love and institutional marriage, will

Human Services, 2021), accessed January 1, 2022, at https://www.cdc.gov/std/statistics/2019/default.htm. See also "The Alarming Rise in STDs, Charted," Advisory Board, August 30, 2018, accessed May 27, 2019, https://www.advisory.com/daily-briefing/2018/08/30/std-cases; Binh Y. Goldstein et al., "High Chlamydia and Gonorrhea Incidence and Reinfection among Performers in the Adult Film Industry," *Sexually Transmitted Diseases* 38, no. 7 (2011): 644–648, accessed May 27, 2019, https://journals.lww.com/stdjournal/Fulltext/2011/07000/High_Chlamydia_and_Gonorrhea_Incidence_and.12.aspx; Marjan Javanbakht et al., "Transmission Behaviors and Prevalence of Chlamydia and Gonorrhea among Adult Film Performers," *Sexually Transmitted Diseases* 44, no. 3 (2017): 181–186, accessed May 27, 2019, https://journals.lww.com/stdjournal/FullText/2017/03000/Transmission_Behaviors_and_Prevalence_of_Chlamydia.10.aspx.

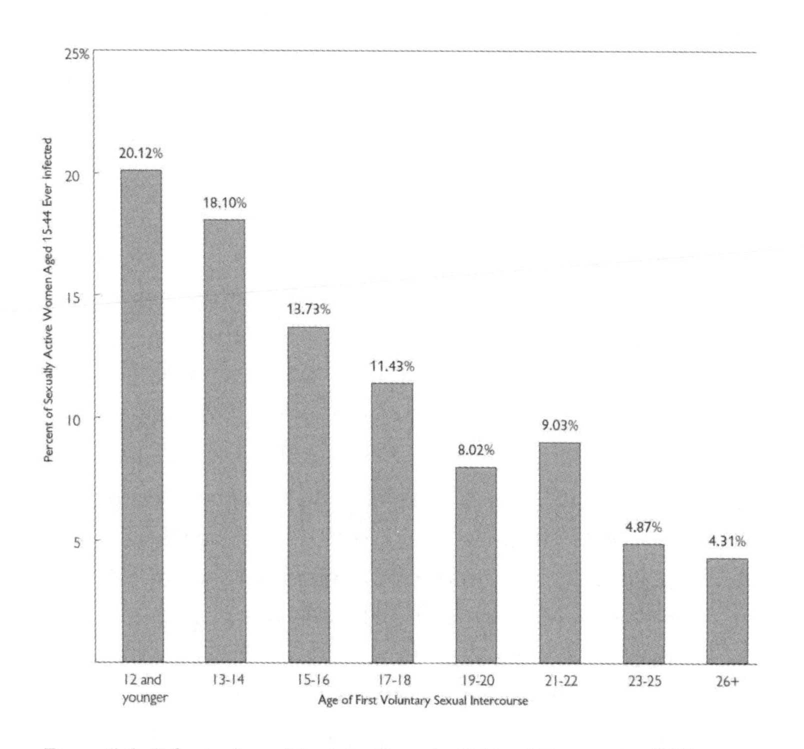

Figure 5.6. Delay in Sexual Activity Cuts the Odds of Contracting STDs.

produce less sexual trauma and will minimize the range of sexual partners and the turmoil associated with the revolving door of sexual partners, as well as the likelihood of contracting a communicable disease. In fact, delay in sexual activity directly manifests the proven variable of less disease. See figure 5.6.[214]

[214] Rector, *Harmful*, 6.

To further highlight this point, a recent 2020 study by the U.S. Department of Health and Human Services clearly supports the natural reduction in sexually transmitted diseases positively caused by delay.[215]

Happiness: Pornography and the Body

With the rise of communicable diseases, increasing rates of sexual addiction and dysfunction, and a generally desensitized population numbed by false pornographic imagery of what sexual activity is normative, it is no wonder that the correlation of happiness to sexual activity is a faulty and irrational finding.[216] If this were so, actors and actresses in the pornography industry would be the happiest people alive, yet the very opposite is true. Studies on the effects of the industry display levels of personal distress, depression, addiction, and suicide that outnumber nearly every occupation and surely the general population. Not surprisingly, the performers suffer from communicable diseases at much higher rates than the general population. In addition, these same allegedly happy performers are rocked by substance abuse problems far exceeding normal measures. As the body mechanically sexualizes itself, as it objectifies its very form and becomes utterly desensitized to normal touch and feel, the actor's resultant need to numb the body becomes unsurprising.[217] The

[215] Rotz, *Assessing the Benefits*.

[216] See Barna Group, *The Porn Phenomenon* (Ventura, CA: Josh McDowell Ministry, 2016), accessed May 27, 2019, http://www.barna.com/wp-content/uploads/2018/12/The-Porn-Phenomenon_excerpt.pdf.

[217] See Corita R. Grudzen and Peter R. Kerndt, "The Adult Film Industry: Time to Regulate?" *PLoS Medicine* 4, no. 6 (June 2007): e126, accessed May 27, 2019, https://www. ncbi.nlm.nih.gov/pmc/articles/PMC1892037.

extent of the negative impacts from this lifestyle is fully catalogued below, in table 5.2,[218] which sweeps away any reasonable conclusion that porn makes for happiness. In fact, the very opposite conclusion is true. Hence, in this context, the body, its sensual experience through sexual activity, cannot create happiness.

Risk of STD by Gender

	Female performers	**Male performers**
HIV and other STD risk		
Communicable diseases	Chlamydia Gonorrhea Herpes HPV HIV/AIDS Hepatitis C	Chlamydia Gonorrhea Herpes HPV HIV/AIDS Hepatitis C
Condom use	Lack of condom use for low and high-risk sexual acts	Lack of condom use for low and high-risk sexual acts
Substance use		
Drugs	Marijuana Methamphetamines Cocaine Valium Opiates	Marijuana

[218] Corita R. Grudzen et al., "Pathways to Health Risk Exposure in Adult Film Performers," *Journal of Urban Health* 86, no. 1 (2009): 67–78, accessed May 27, 2019, https://www.ncbi.nlm.nih.gov/pmc/articles/PMC2629520/table/Tab2/?report=objectonly.

	Female performers	**Male performers**
Alcohol	Underage drinking among <21-year-old performers	Drinking on the set
Body enhancement		
Surgical	Breast augmentation Vaginal surgery/ reconstruction Other cosmetic surgery	Hair implants Penis extensions
Medical	Self-administering enemas Tanning Excessive dieting and exercise	Taking Viagra Tanning Excessive dieting and exercise
Risk of physical trauma		
General	Chemical burns from sex toys Anal tears Cuts and bruises Being slapped, having hair pulled on set by other performers Asphyxiation Simulating rape or violence in the scene	Wounds due to penile injections

	Female performers	**Male performers**
Sex acts	Vaginal sex Anal sex Double-vaginal penetration Double-anal penetration Simultaneous double penetration (vaginal and anal) “Gang bang”: 1 woman has >2 sexual partners one after the other	Vaginal sex Simultaneous double-vaginal penetration Simultaneous double-anal penetration
Mental health risk		
Clinically diagnosed	Depression Suicide Schizophrenia Bipolar disorder Anxiety disorders Post-traumatic stress disorder	Depression Suicide
General symptoms	Anxiety Stress Low self-esteem Poor body image	Anxiety Stress Low self-esteem Poor body image Sex addiction

	Female performers	**Male performers**
Financial risks		
Finances	Adopting patterns of increased consumption of materials and goods Having children, partners, or other family members to support	Males earn less relative to females for same sexual acts
Contracts/ negotiations	Being offered increasing amounts of money for higher risk sex acts No royalties from movies Agents controlling contract terms and/or payment Female performers eventually make less money for the same acts, making it necessary to do more scenes to maintain the same lifestyle	Being offered increasing amounts of money for higher risk sex acts No royalties from movies Agents controlling contract terms and/or payment

	Female performers	**Male performers**
Social interactions		
Relationships in the industry	Immersion in adult industry social networks, leaving behind other supportive family and friends outside the industry	Immersion in adult industry social networks, leaving behind other supportive family and friends outside the industry
	Agents control female performers: provide clothes, trips, car services to sets in exchange for more work	
	Forcing or coercing female performers into sex acts	
	Sex with agents, directors, or producers to get work ("couch casting")	

Table 5.2. Risk of STD by Gender.

In 2017–2018, the porn industry experienced suicide rates among its participants at levels never before encountered. Acting as if none of this was predictable or expected, the industry launched into a series of investigations and self-inquiring studies trying to discern the cause of young actresses killing themselves at alarming rates. Using terms like *tragedy*, *shocking*, *preventable*, the pornography business, which sells the body and sex as the elixir for happiness, generates the opposite results. Rampant drug usage dominates the workplace, even to the point that drugs are central to the industry's own productions. Disease, depression, estrangement, and isolation all devastate its participants. In fact, the entire entertainment industry has been rocked by increasing levels of drug usage over the last few decades. The National Institutes of Health charts this undeniable upward swing in figure 5.7.[219]

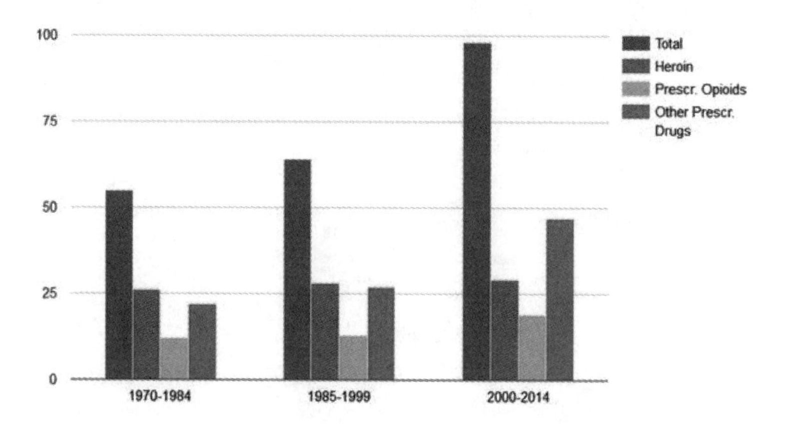

Figure 5.7. Drug Use Increase, 1970–2014.

All of this demonstrates the absolute futility of looking to the body or sexuality as a basis for human happiness or contentment.[220]

Despite this trauma, some former performers in the industry prove that there is redemption and salvation. No greater example

[219] See Johannes M. Just et al., "Drug-Related Celebrity Deaths: A Cross-Sectional Study," *Substance Abuse Treatment and Prevention Policy* 11 (2016): 40, accessed May 27, 2019, https://www.ncbi.nlm.nih.gov/pmc/articles/PMC5148833.

[220] Vanessa Arba, "The Shocking Information the Porn Industry Doesn't Want You to Know," Adventist News Network, August 1, 2021, accessed January 1, 2022, at https://adventist.news/news/the-shocking-information-the-porn-industry-doesnt-want-you-to-know.

of this proof of the sordid lifestyle rampant in the adult porn industry, and the discovery of faith and redemption in Christ, exists than the story of Brittni De La Mora. Now a Christian pastor, she is dedicated to helping those enslaved in a world she once thought she was permanently lost in.[221]

Happiness: The Body and Sexual Promiscuity

Aristotle

Take the incontinent person exceeding the limits of right reason because of passion that so overcomes him that he does not act according to right reason; still he is not convinced that he should abandon himself to such pleasures without restriction.[222]

Aquinas

When the lower powers are strongly moved toward their object, the result is that the higher powers are hindered and disordered in their acts. Now the effect of the vice of lust is that the lower appetite, namely the concupiscible, is most vehemently intent on its object.[223]

No matter where the question of happiness arises, relative to the body or sensory experiences, inadequacy and impossibility

[221] Brittni De La Mora's remarkable work can be discovered at https://www.instagram.com/brittnidelamora.

[222] *Nic. Ethics*, 1151a20–28.

[223] Aquinas, *Summa*, II–II, q. 153, art. 5.

emerge. As both Aristotle and Aquinas repeatedly make plain, the idea of meaningful happiness cannot depend on the corruptible, temporary, and very changeable body, nor can it rely on the transiency of sensory experiences—in touch, taste, smell, or sight. In these cases, the pleasure experienced, if in a proper desire or appetite, will be even more fleeting than our bodily state.

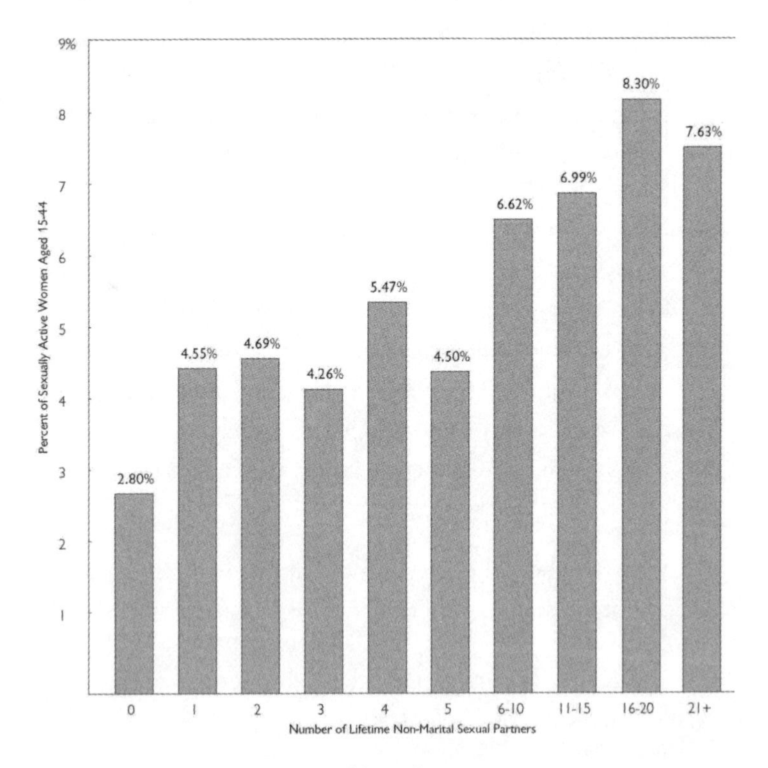

Figure 5.8. Women, Depression, and Sexual Activity.

And pleasure, which underlies the appetitive and sensory delight conducive to positive views of sexual activity, which fosters procreation and the propagation of the species, is not an evil or horrid thing in the minds of Aristotle and Aquinas. Sexual pleasure, as with all other forms of human pleasure, need be in the virtuous mean, so to speak, and not suffer from inordinate desire or affection, nor should it enslave the human agent or provide occasions for obsessive or compulsive behavior. Most crucially, sexual pleasure must remain within some set of boundaries, some organized parameters such as marriage and family life, and be open to the possibility of new life—children that add to the familial structure. Pleasure here is consistent with happiness. In contrast, pleasure anywhere, with anyone at any time, leads to a vacant morality based on self-pleasure for its own sake. In this latter category, there will never be happiness but rather distress and alienation. The Heritage Foundation graphically portrays the heavy price that promiscuity demands of the agent choosing the lifestyle. For example, the foundation correlated female depression levels with the count of sexual partners. Hence as the number of partners increases, so too do the level and depth of depression. See figure 5.8.[224]

The esteemed Mayo Clinic reaches similar conclusions on the mental health decline caused by excessive and compulsive sexual activity.[225]

None of this is really all that startling, for our makeup, our nature and essence, is not wired for such objectified indifference to others or such callous intimacy.

[224] Rector, *Harmful*, 21.

[225] See "Compulsive Sexual Behavior," Mayo Clinic, February 7, 2020, accessed January 1, 2022, at https://www.mayoclinic.org/diseases-conditions/compulsive-sexual-behavior/symptoms-causes/syc-20360434.

Similar findings were discovered in teenage males and females, which is that higher levels of depression and increased suicide attempts accompanied higher incidences of sexual activity and promiscuity (see table 5.3 and figures 5.9 and 5.10).[226]

Depression and Sexual Activity				
	Never/ Rarely Depressed	Depressed Sometimes	Depressed a Lot	Depressed Most/ All of the Time
BOYS 14-17				
Sexually Active	63.3%	28.4%	5%	3.3%
Not Sexually Active	76.2%	20.3%	2.6%	0.8%
GIRLS 14-17				
Sexually Active	36.8%	37.9%	15.5%	9.8%
Not sexually active	60.2%	32.1%	4.9%	2.8%

Table 5.3. Depression and Sexual Activity.

[226] Rector, *Harmful*, 3–4.

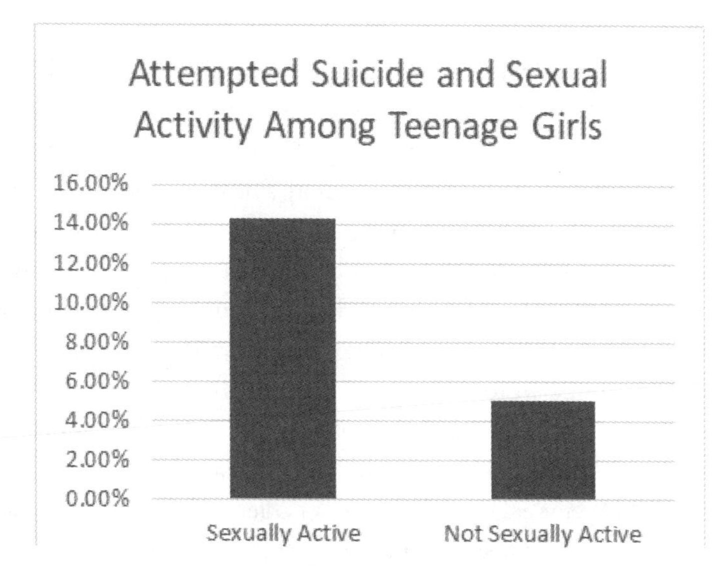

Figure 5.9. Attempted Suicide and Sexual Activity in Teenage Girls.

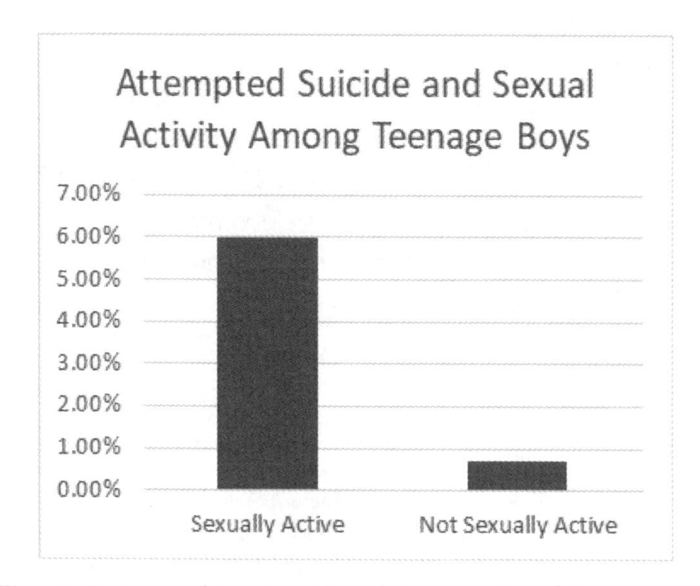

Figure 5.10. Attempted Suicide and Sexual Activity in Teenage Boys.

A 2017 study from the Canadian National Institute of Health indicates that some parties employ sexual promiscuity as a coping mechanism in cases of depression.[227] By *coping* we mean the masking of other issues, whether depression, suicidal thoughts, or some other pain. This type of masking emulates and imitates the use of drugs and alcohol to soften the hurt and the trauma a person has experienced. The effects are predictably contrary, for whether it be sex, drugs, or alcohol masking the hurt and harm, the use of these techniques produces a far worse result in the human person. To be sure, sex, drugs, and alcohol heighten rather than minimize the sadness, the depression, and the suicidal thoughts. Further, as the behavior engaged in becomes riskier and more extreme, so also the problems become increasingly severe, and any chance at happiness evaporates by the conduct.

Aristotle

> But some pleasures are necessary, others not necessary; some are necessary up to a point, while excesses and defects are not necessary at all.... Hence a man is called intemperate who pursues excesses in pleasures by desiring them beyond measure or by deliberately choosing them for their own sake and not the sake of something else.[228]

[227] Cecilia Fredlund et al., "Self-Reported Frequency of Sex as Self-Injury (SASI) in a National Study of Swedish Adolescents and Association to Sociodemographic Factors, Sexual Behaviors, Abuse and Mental Health," *Child and Adolescent Psychiatry and Mental Health* 11 (2017): 9, accessed May 27, 2019, https://www.ncbi.nlm.nih.gov/pmc/articles/PMC5331746.

[228] *Nic. Ethics*, 1150a13–16.

Aquinas

The fornicator is said to sin against his own body, not merely because the pleasure of fornication is consummated in the flesh ... but also because he acts against the good of his own body by an undue resolution and defilement ... and an undue association with another.[229]

The *American Journal of Preventive Medicine* tracked and calculated this reality in its assessment of data provided in a national "Youth Risk Behavior Surveillance Survey." Not surprisingly, the more perverse and serious the sex, drugs, and alcohol misuse becomes, the greater the degree of depression. For some sobering statistics on various risky behaviors and their outcomes in adolescents, read the article "Which Comes First in Adolescence—Sex and Drugs or Depression?"[230]

Studies on college students and casual sexuality with multiple partners generally lead to similar conclusions. The mere quality of being "casual" about the intimate sexual act seems a contradiction in terms. Even so, the terms applied to sexual exchange—such as "hookup," "one-night stands," or "on the hunt or prowl"—highlight the temporality and fleetingness of these exchanges. There are other ways of describing this casualness, and research indicates that conducting sexual affairs in this fashion generates negative reactions, ranging from "sexual regret" to abject remorse over the insignificant way in which sexuality is treated:

[229] Aquinas, *Summa*, I-II, q. 154, art. 2.

[230] Denise D. Hallfors et al., "Which Comes First in Adolescence—Sex and Drugs or Depression?" *American Journal of Preventive Medicine* 29, no. 3 (2005): 163–170.

- In the month before the study, 18.6 percent of men and 7.4 percent of women reported at least one sexual encounter.
- Those who had recently had casual sex reported lower levels of self-esteem, life satisfaction, psychological, and eudaimonic well-being than those who had not had casual sex.
- Those who had casual sex reported higher levels of depression and social and general anxiety than those who had not.[231]

In a sense, this is a commentary on the disposability of even sexuality as if a commercial product or a foodstuff. Human activity, in a sexual sense, has very few rivals due to its intimacy, its power and capacity to procreate, and its ability to foster a greater or higher love than the erotic experience that can never be as perpetual as charity and love of person can make possible. The "one-night stand" culture is utterly desolate. There is a "positive correlation between casual sex and psychological stress and diminished well-being."[232]

Aristotle

How is it that no one can feel pleasure continuously? Is it from fatigue? Certainly no creature with a body is capable of uninterrupted activity. Therefore pleasure is also not continuous, for it accompanies activity.[233]

[231] Bersamin, "Business," 49.

[232] Ibid; See also Sophie Dubé et al., "Consequences of Casual Sex Relationships and Experiences on Adolescents' Psychological Well-Being: A Prospective Study," *Journal of Sex Research* 54, no. 8 (October 2017): 1006–1017, accessed May 27, 2019, https://www.ncbi.nlm.nih.gov/pmc/articles/PMC5731847.

[233] *Nic. Ethics*, 1174a3–6.

Aquinas

We must add ... the pleasure of conjugal [marital] intercourse has no moral malice, since it is neither a mortal nor a venial sin.[234]

Happiness: The Body and Drugs/Alcohol

Contemporary life is laden with a myriad of social and moral ills, all of which undermine the pursuit of a happy life and contented state. The rationales for illicit drug usage and even licit overuse, as well as alcohol abuse, generally fall into three categories according to the National Institute of Drug Abuse.

First, people want to feel good. Taking a drug can feel really good for a short time. That's why people keep taking them—to have those good feelings again and again. But even though someone can take more and more of a drug, the good feelings don't last. Soon the person is taking the drug just to keep from feeling bad.

Second, people want to stop feeling bad. Some who feel very worried, afraid, or sad use drugs to try to stop feeling so awful. This doesn't really help their problems and can lead to addiction, which can make them feel much worse.

Third, people want to do well in school or at work. Some individuals who want to get good grades, get a better job, or earn more money might think drugs will give them more energy, keep them awake, or make them think faster. But it usually doesn't work. It also may put their health at risk and can lead to addiction.[235]

[234] Aquinas, *Summa*, I–II. q. 34, art. 1, ad 1.

[235] See Brittany A. Bugbee et al., "Substance Use, Academic Performance, and Academic Engagement among High School Seniors," *Journal of School Health* 89, no. 2 (2019), accessed July 18, 2022, https://onlinelibrary.wiley.com/doi/10.1111/josh.12723.

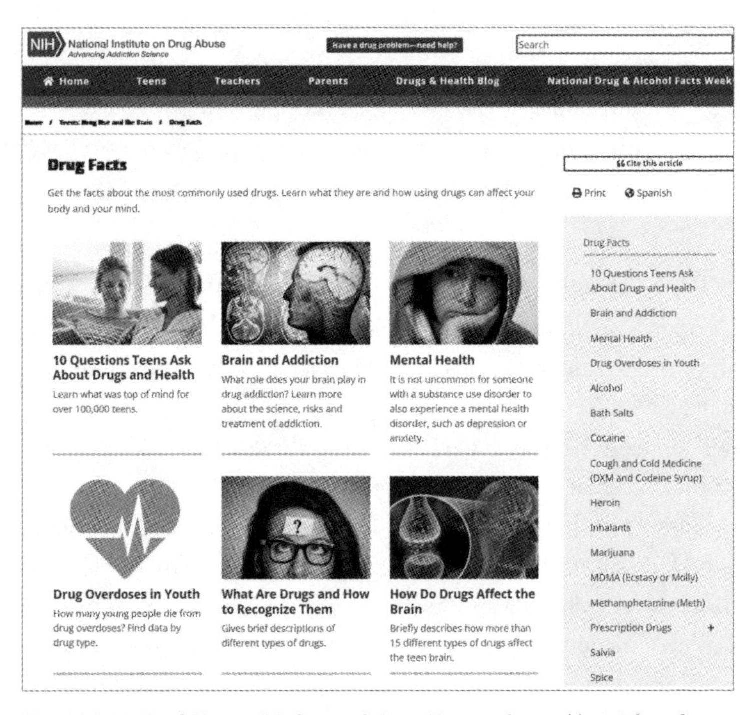

Figure 5.11. Find Easy-to-Understand Drug Facts at https://teens.drugabuse.gov/teens/drug-facts.

Within these faulty justifications appears the ironic puzzle that the person hopes, wants, and needs to be and feel happy while at the same time they adopt behaviors guaranteed to produce the opposite result. And even when intellectually concluding that this irony be true, the drug user, in his or her zeal for the next high, simply repeats the same absurd behavior and descends further downward. See figure 5.11.[236]

In this way, vice dominates the mind of the person; vice shapes and habituates as if command or law, and vice inherent in drug

[236] "Easy-to-Read Drug Facts," National Institute of Drug Abuse, easyread.drugabuse.gov, accessed May 27, 2019.

and alcohol abuse culminates in the destruction of one's mind, spirit, and body. During the age of Aristotle and Aquinas, neither encountered the scourge of synthetic drugs to which we have become accustomed, although drunkenness could be in full bloom.

Aristotle

Every excess of vice, for example, folly, timidity, intemperance, and harshness is either brutish or caused by sickness.[237]

Aquinas

The good of reason is hindered in two ways: in one way by that which is contrary to reason, in another by that which takes away the use of reason. Now that which is contrary to reason has more the character of an evil than that which takes away the use of reason for a time, since the use of reason, which is taken away by drunkenness may be either good or evil, whereas the goods of virtue, which are taken away by things that are contrary to reason, are always good.[238]

Each of these behaviors also challenges the person in more than moral terms since addiction is and does become an additional physical reality the user must contend with. It is simply too easy to argue that the users are lacking in moral reasoning. The acute addictive qualities of heroin, meth, cocaine, and the new synthetic fentanyl generate addiction rates and outcomes not seen

[237] *Nic. Ethics*, 1149a4–7.

[238] Aquinas, *Summa*, II–II, q. 150, art. 3.

[Data are based on household interviews of a sample of the civilian noninstitutionalized population aged 12 and over]

Characteristic	Any illicit drug[1]			Marijuana			Misuse of prescription psychotherapeutic drugs[2]		
	2002	2017	2018	2002	2017	2018	2002	2017	2018
Age group				Percent of population					
12 years and over	---	11.2	11.7	6.2	9.6	10.1	---	2.2	2.0
12–13 years	---	2.0	2.1	1.4	0.7	0.9	---	0.5	0.4
14–15 years	---	6.3	6.7	7.6	5.0	5.1	---	1.3	1.0
16–17 years	---	14.8	14.8	15.7	13.2	13.5	---	2.5	2.3
18–25 years	---	24.2	23.9	17.3	22.1	22.1	---	4.5	3.7
26–34 years	---	17.4	18.9	7.7	14.8	16.7	---	3.7	3.2
35 years and over	---	7.7	8.1	3.1	6.3	6.7	---	1.5	1.5

Figure 5.12. Use of Drugs, Individuals Aged Twelve and Over.

from alcohol alone. It is a picture that has steadily and consistently become more miserable since the early 2000s, with pharmacological reliance and alcohol usage rising across all ethnic groups and age brackets. The CDC charts this negative portrayal. See figure 5.12.[239]

Even though we know the negative effects of so many behaviors that cause a certain slavishness to immorality, the culture, the modern media, and the intelligentsia in universities and high society continue to exhort our "liberation" from the shackles of moral propriety. Coming a long way from the "hippie days" mantra—"if it feels good, it must be right" or "love the one you're with"—the current depravity evident in these present days makes one almost nostalgic. With an unrivaled crisis in modern Catholicism—where the leaders of the world's oldest religious denomination have so lost their bearings they are not repulsed by pedophilia, the immoral lifestyles promoted in the media culture, or our current legislative craze to legalize and decriminalize one conduct after another,

[239] Center for Behavioral Health Statistics and Quality, "National Survey on Drug Use and Health (NSDUH)," Substance Abuse and Mental Health Services Administration. Available from https://www.samhsa.gov/data/population-data-nsduh and unpublished data provided by NSDUH. See Appendix I, National Survey on Drug Use and Health (NSDUH), accessed January 1, 2022, at https://www.cdc.gov/nchs/data/hus/2019/020-508.pdf.

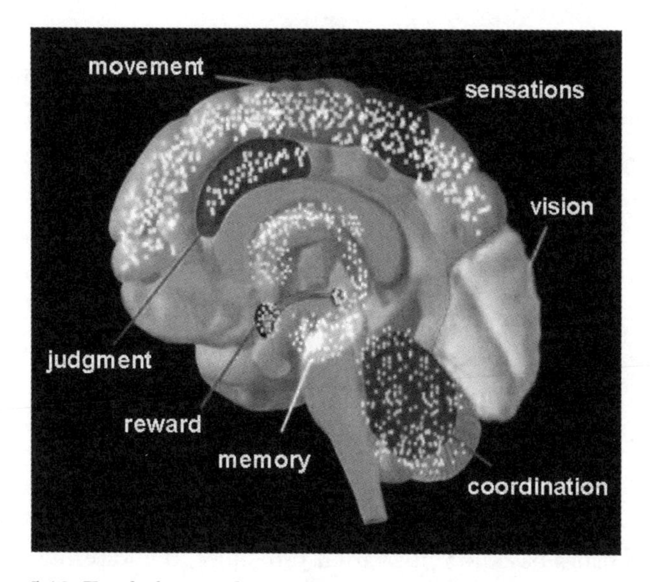

Figure 5.13. Tetrahydrocannabinol (THC) Impacts Marked in Yellow from Marijuana Use.

especially involving drugs—is it any wonder that happiness is in short supply? The signs of cultural rupture and fissure are simply undeniable. When legislators recently called for legalized infanticide in third-trimester abortion, concerned citizens on the left and the right were struck by this new radicality. And with efforts to decriminalize marijuana now running at full bore, with the legalization of other drugs, like "magic mushrooms," soon to follow, one wonders about our collective sanity. Even the false and misleading claims that marijuana has little, if any, medical or mental impacts on its users have shown no loss of luster in the public eye. The impact on human neurology alone is worth the avoidance (see figure 5.13).[240]

[240] "Cannabis (Marijuana) DrugFacts," National Institute on Drug Abuse,accessed May 27, 2019, https://www.drugabuse.gov/publications/drugfacts/marijuana.

Other negative impacts of the allegedly harmless marijuana belie the push for legalization and include but certainly are not limited to:

- altered senses (e.g., seeing brighter colors)
- altered sense of time
- changes in mood
- impaired body movement
- difficulty with thinking and problem-solving
- impaired memory
- hallucinations (when taken in high doses)
- delusions (when taken in high doses)
- psychosis (when taken in high doses)[241]

Couple this legislative outrage with the decriminalization of hard drugs based on libertarian principles, the lowering of the statutory rape age, the softening of religious rights and their protection, and the bizarre push for "socialism" when history resolutely demonstrates its inherent failure—one has a recipe for social and cultural turbulence. We live in crazy times; more compellingly, we live in times where happiness is in short supply. From 2015 to the present, the rates for drug-induced deaths are rising at staggering rates. Pennsylvania alone, by way of illustration, suffers the pathology of drug usage in literally every county (see figure 5.14).[242]

The target audience for these deaths are primarily younger and more youthful figures who should be in the prime of their lives but are instead captive to the false and artificial happiness these drugs provide. The numbers speak for themselves (see figure 5.15).[243]

[241] Ibid.

[242] DEA Philadelphia Division and University of Pittsburgh, *The Opioid Threat in Pennsylvania* (2018), https://www.dea.gov/sites/default/files/2018-10/PA%20Opioid%20Report%20Final%20FINAL.pdf.

[243] Ibid.

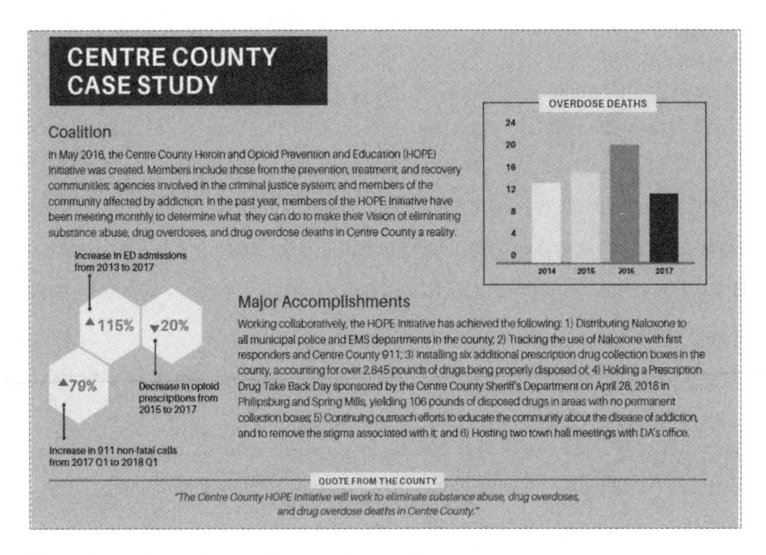

Figure 5.14. Drug Use in Centre County, PA.

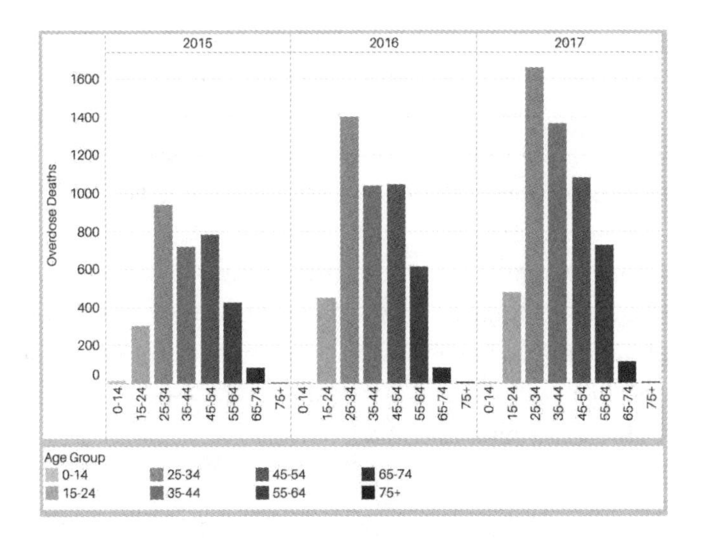

Figure 5.15. Age Distribution of Drug-Related Overdoses in PA, 2015–2017.

The data from the Partnership to End Addiction lay out a prophetic picture of how early usage of alcohol and drugs almost guarantees later-in-life abuse problems—in the same way that earlier sexual histories appear to lead to later difficulties and dysfunction in marriage and sexuality. The National Center for Drug Addiction states that more than 90 percent of people with a substance problem began smoking, drinking, or using other drugs before age eighteen.[244]

The craving for drugs and alcohol, for the temporary high or false sense of happiness, has now reached epidemic proportions throughout the country. It is almost as if no one can live naturally, without the aid of some prop-up or other artifice to buttress happiness, whether it be excessive drinking, opioid painkiller abuse, even antidepressants—those pills to make a person happy. With all these synthetic recipes and formulas for happiness, why is happiness in such short supply?

Aside from historic heroin addiction, the use of cocaine and crystal meth has accelerated due to the fast-acting nature of these drugs. Add intensely addictive qualities to the same, and one encounters an almost satanic substance. In the case of meth, the bodily destruction is beyond striking—where the face and body literally become disfigured.

Happiness finds no solace in either drug or alcohol abuse. In each setting the human person falters in his or her own personal development, character development, and overall flourishing. Instead of growth there is backsliding in all aspects of human life—physically, spiritually, and intellectually.

[244] "Fast Facts about Addiction," Partnership to End Addiciton, accessed July 18, 2022, https://drugfree.org/article/fast-facts-about-addiction/.

Aristotle

But not all pleasures of this kind are good, because some are shameful and dishonorable while others are harmful, causing sickness.[245]

Aquinas

Man is more prone to sins of intemperance, because ... pleasures are connatural to us, and for this reason these sins are said to find greatest favor with the devil, for not being graver than other sins, but, because they occur more frequently among men.[246]

In the final analysis, excessive and slavish usage of alcohol and drugs cannot lead any human agent to happiness as defined throughout this text. Indeed, its usage fosters and nurtures the result most contrary to that happiness that its users sought. Since happiness depends upon moral excellence and a life well lived—in accordance with our fundamental natures and the choice of human activities that direct us to our proper end and goal, as well as our ultimate end—the abuse and use of drugs, whether legal or not, hinders that plan for living.

Conclusion

By now it is readily apparent that the body is incapable of providing true happiness. To be certain, a body does provide avenues

[245] *Nic. Ethics*, 1152b20–22.

[246] Aquinas, *Summa*, II–II, q. 150, art. 3.

for sensory and intellectual pleasure. It should also be noted that pleasures, in the world of Aristotle and Aquinas, are not dirty words or activities to be avoided. In fact, pleasure is "connatural" to us but not a version of pleasure without restriction or selected parameters. Hence, this chapter, once done looking to the impossibility of the body being our ultimate end, concentrates on whether certain activities of the body might deliver perfect happiness. More specifically, does sexuality produce perfect happiness? Will pornography and promiscuity, either by direct or indirect participation, make people happy or at least happier? Finally, will alcohol and drug activities lead to a more contented place? In each of these queries, we can respond with a resounding no, because none of these human movements generate anything more than a temporary sensory delight. When a person practices these activities in the extreme, such as in a drunken, debauchery-filled, drug-induced lifestyle, happiness shall find no home. When sexuality is reduced to a numbers game or a promiscuous series of sexual exchanges, the alienation and loneliness that arise from this objectified view of human dignity surely open no avenue for human happiness. Aquinas argues that a life of sexual promiscuity is "contrary to the good of the human race"[247] and "contrary to the love of our neighbor."[248] Aristotle and Aquinas posit uniform conclusions as to what will constitute happiness in matters of the body and pleasure, namely:

1. The body cannot lead to happiness.
2. Pleasure of the body tied to sensory experience cannot lead to happiness.
3. Alcohol and drug usage never nurture happiness.

[247] Aquinas, *Summa*, II–II, q. 154, art. 3.

[248] Ibid.

Rules for a Happy Life

5.0: That Happiness Cannot Be Discovered in the Body

5.1: That Happiness Cannot Be Achieved in Sensory Pleasure Alone

5.2: That Happiness and Pleasure, When Guided to Proper Goods and Ends, Are Suitable

5.3: That Happiness Depends on the Body, the Mind, and the Spirit of the Human Person

5.4: That Happiness, in Its Fullest and Most Complete State, Is Grounded in the Spirit

5.5: That Happiness Seeks the Incorporeal in the Perfection and Beatific Vision of God

5.6: That Happiness and Sexuality, in the Proper Parameters of Marriage and Procreation, Are Compatible

5.7: That Happiness, Inordinate Sexual Lust, Promiscuity, and a Lack of Chastity Are Contrary States

5.8: That Happiness and Artificial, Cosmetic Manipulation of the Body Are Inconsistent Acts

5.9: That Happiness Cannot Be Fostered or Nurtured by Drug Usage and Addictive Behavior

5.10: That Happiness Is Promoted by Living Naturally and in Accordance with Our Natures

5.11: That Happiness Arising from the Body Is Impossible Due to Its Corruptibility

5.12: That Happiness Is Rooted Not in Feelings or Appetites but in the Human Soul and Reason

6

Happiness: Family, Relationships, Marriage, and Children

Introduction

By nature, human beings are social and political creatures, an observation made by Aristotle in his political analysis. None of us are born to be isolated or alienated from others, and as history demonstrates, human existence always tends to the collective, not the isolated, way of being. For Aquinas, belonging to a community, as a social being, was part of our natural law imprint.

Aristotle

> But he who is unable to live in society, or who has no need because he is sufficient for himself, must either be a beast or a god; he is not part of the state. A social instinct is implanted in all men by nature.[249]

[249] Aristotle, *Pol.*, 1253a25–35.

Aquinas

But since man is naturally a civic and social animal ... whereby man is directed in relation to other men among whom he is to dwell.[250]

Aside from the clear evidence of communal existence being the preferred and most natural form for human life, the reverse imagery of a common good, collective mentality always gives cause to be concerned. When mass murderers, serial sexual predators, and sociopathic individuals are encountered, they generally leave behind extraordinary human wreckage and act for ends and goals inconsistent with a flourishing and happy life. People like Ted Kaczynski, a.k.a. the Unabomber, and Jeffrey Dahmer, the serial killer and sexual degenerate, to name but two, lived life in general isolation from others and repelled the very natural associational contexts that are quite evident in human society. In the case of Ted Kaczynski, we encounter an antisocial streak that manifests his disturbed relations with the world and his neighbors. Living in isolation in Montana, the Unabomber was personally responsible for death and mayhem at very high levels, building and sending untraceable bombs to random targets and intentionally leaving false clues to throw off authorities (see figures 6.1 and 6.2).

The Unabomber was the classic loner and isolationist, utterly mad at the entire world and seeking every means to escape normal human interaction.

To be isolated from others is an abnormal state for our natural constitution and instincts, as well as our natural law, which

[250] Aquinas, *Summa*, I–II, q. 72, art. 4, corp.

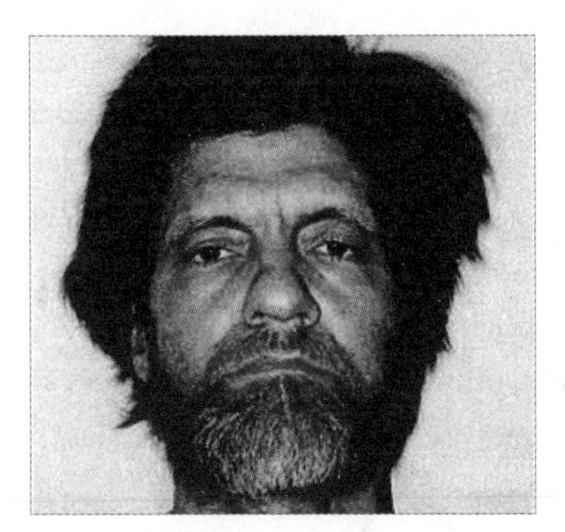

Figure 6.1. The Unabomber. Courtesy of the FBI.

Figure 6.2. The Unabomber's Montana Home. Courtesy of the FBI.

commands a life with others, an associational existence in a host of contexts—from family to service for and to others—and an intimate relationship with God. And while we should not adopt all things in the material world as our purpose, we must integrate our life fully into a social and communal setting. Contrary, isolationist attitudes are truly destructive and often discerned in this nation's returning soldiers and veterans—especially those burdened with multiple deployments into our current war zones. Feeling estranged, alienated from others, and perpetually questioning life and its meaning, soldiers have suicide and depression rates that are further exacerbated by poor relationship skills and a sense that no one really understands or cares.[251]

The VA and other governmental entities, as well as private charities, have targeted this group for its terrible suicide rate. The VA uses a self-screening tool for predictive purposes. Visit the VA's My HealtheVet website to browse their various screening tools at https://www.myhealth.va.gov/mhv-portal-web/web/myhealthevet/home.[252] See figure 6.3.[253]

Whether for distressed soldiers or forlorn laypeople, the path to happiness does not follow any road to isolation or estrangement and instead compels human interaction and human institutions that value each and every person.

In Aquinas, the tenets of the natural law, those inclinations imprinted in our very being by the Creator, demonstrate the normalcy of human interaction. Aside from our desire to live in a community, parents instinctually want to care for offspring. For that matter, the predisposition to propagate the species and to engage in sexual intercourse for procreative purposes appears about as natural as it gets and as intimate as a relationship can be. Our very preservation as a species depends upon continuous physical,

[251] Mike Richman, "The Loneliness Factor: How Much Does It Drive Depression in Veterans?," U.S. Department of Veterans Affairs, February 28, 2018, accessed May 27, 2019, https://www.research.va.gov/currents/0218-The-loneliness-factor-in-depression.cfm.

[252] See also ibid.

[253] See also Harvard Medical School and HelpGuide, accessed May 27, 2019, https://www.helpguide.org/harvard.htm.

Figure 6.3. Post-traumatic Stress Disorder Is a Significant or Extreme Emotional or Psychological Response to a Shocking, Dangerous, or Traumatic Event. It Affects Approximately 7 percent of the U.S. Population and 12–18 percent of Combat Veterans Deployed to Iraq and Afghanistan. U.S. Air Force photo by Senior Airman Christian Clausen/Released.

mental, and emotional interaction with other beings. As Aristotle and Aquinas observe, this social and communal quality is not second nature to us but in fact is our nature precisely.

Aristotle

Now, that man is more of a political animal than bees or any other gregarious animals is evident.... And it is a characteristic of man that he alone has any sense of good and evil, of just and unjust, and the like, and the association of living beings who have this sense makes a family and a state.[254]

[254] *Pol.*, 1153a5–20.

Aquinas

> Thus man has a natural inclination to know the truth about God, and to live in society.... For instance to shun ignorance, to avoid offending those among whom he has to live.[255]

An eighty-year study from Harvard University has repeatedly proven that our capacity to garner happiness depends on a wide variety of factors, although our sense of family and community is continuously important. One of the study's chief researchers notes that "loneliness kills" and it is as "powerful as smoking or alcoholism."[256] Happiness will not be possible in any environment characterized by isolation or alienation from others. This longitudinal study makes plain that "close relationships, more than money or fame, are what keep people happy throughout their lives."[257]

The stresses and strains associated with loneliness and human estrangement undercut happiness. To be alone is to be in a dire state. To be isolated is to assure a depressive mantra that self cannot cure or resolve. While there is no specific formula for human activity and human interaction that fulfills, there are common traits and attributes that seem to foster more happiness than not. What is clear, from the empirical and anecdotal evidence, is that long-term marriages and longer, happier lives are correlated. And the same also could be said about the role, scope, and size of families and offspring to that marriage.

[255] Aquinas, *Summa*, I–II, q. 94, art. 2, corp.

[256] Liz Mineo, "Good Genes Are Nice, but Joy Is Better," *The Harvard Gazette*, April 11, 2017, 4.

[257] Ibid., 3.

Yet this primary imagery of family is not the sole or exclusive means to social, communal, and personal integration, which in turn triggers higher rates of happiness. For those that give their lives to others—for example, sisters and religious orders that educate children, nurse the sick and the feeble, and care for the poor and disaffected—seem by most accounts to be much happier than the self-serving, narcissistic materialist who knows nothing other than self. In the next chapter of this text, we shall examine the longevity of religious nuns, their health, both mental and physical, when compared to other occupations, and their quotient of happiness. While these nuns are neither married nor have children, their targeted audience for the services they so passionately and charitably provide becomes another avenue for the joy that emerges when giving to others and fully integrating oneself into the world at large.

The point here is that the cookie cutter toward a happy life, in regard to social and communal living, has many shapes and sizes—although the common thread witnessed among the happier versions is the love of others that is so freely exhibited. Teachers, nurses, doctors, and lawyers, to name just a few—all have this fantastic capacity to make exceptional contributions to the social order, as does the accountant who reads books to children from distressed communities, or the plumber who fixes an elderly citizen's house free of charge because he cares. Acts of charity and selflessness are the antidote to a lonely and distressed life. In this way, acts of love and charity are always relational and dependent on others, and the more attentive we are to others, the greater sense of personal satisfaction and happiness one achieves.[258] This does not arise from a life of purposeful isolation but instead from a conscious choice to integrate oneself

[258] Christian Smith, *The Paradox of Generosity: Giving We Receive, Grasping We Lose* (Oxford: Oxford University Press, 2014).

into the world around us. As Jesus of Nazareth stated in the New Testament, in the book of Luke, "Give, and it shall be given to you: good measure and pressed down and shaken together and running over shall they give into your bosom. For with the same measure that you shall mete withal, it shall be measured to you again."[259]

Aristotle

For friendship is a virtue … and also it is one of the most indispensable requirements of life. For no one would choose to live without friends, but possessing all other good things.… And in poverty or any other misfortune men think friends are their only resource. Friends are an aid to the young, to guard them from error; to the elderly, to tend them, and to supplement their failing powers of action; to those in the prime of life, to assist them in noble deeds.… And the affection of parent for offspring and of offspring for parent seems to be a natural instinct, not only in man but also in birds and in most animals; as also is friendship between members of the same species.[260]

Aquinas

Friendship extends to a person in two ways: first in respect of himself, and in this way friendship never extends but to one's friends: secondly, it extends to someone in respect of another, as, when a man has friendship for a certain person, for his sake he loves all belonging to

[259] Luke 6:38.
[260] *Pol.*, 1155a10–20.

> him, be they children, servants, or connected with him in any way. Indeed, so much do we love our friends, that for their sake we love all who belong to them, even if they hurt or hate us; so that, in this way, the friendship of charity extends even to our enemies, whom we love out of charity in relation to God, to Whom the friendship of charity is chiefly directed.[261]

Happiness, Marriage, and Family

The importance of the marital state and the familial structure is a central theme in both Aristotle and Aquinas, although their emphasis on why is slightly different. In Aquinas, the idea of family and marriage rests at the center of his natural law theory, and, at the same time, both marriage and family have a political element relative to the common good of any society. Strong families and strong marital bonds produce strong communities. In addition, Aquinas treats marriage and family in theological terms too, holding that marriage is a sacrament labeled Matrimony and its purpose is driven toward other natural law instincts like propagation, procreation, care of offspring, and the overall education of children. This basic, most fundamental of insights, which recognizes the need for a formal, familial structure, is more enlightened than much of modern social and behavioral science—disciplines that appear unable to connect these basic dots—that strong families, with loving parents, formally united in marriage, lead to happy and successful children.[262]

[261] Aquinas, *Summa*, II–II, q. 23, art. 1, ad 2.

[262] See Robert Slavin, "St. Thomas and His Teaching on the Family," *Dominicana* 18, no. 3 (1933), accessed May 27, 2019, https://www.

To the contemporary theorist, the idea of marriage and family reflects mere convention rather than a substantive purpose, and, at the same time, the need to be married becomes irrelevant to those that really "love" one another. Add to this a host of other challenges to family structure, like the feminist critique on the lack of any urgent need for fathers or men in the family; the idea that divorce, adultery, and unfaithfulness have no impact on children or the institution of marriage; or the current euphoria on gender roles, same-sex marriage, and the other structural contortions on traditional family having absolutely no impact on the sanctity, integrity, and stability of the marital state and its offspring. In some ways, the sheer volume of social challenges to traditional marriage and family makes sorting it all out an impossibility.[263]

One of the most commonly heard rationales for all of these marital and family machinations is the motto Love Is Love. Hence, whoever "loves" one another in whatever form or leveling of partners is the new measure for what love really is. In the world of Aristotle and Aquinas this is patently absurd, for love and charity, like all the other virtues, must be in accord with reason, with our basic nature and inclinations. Love is not simply an emotive feeling or a sensual, sensory reaction to another but something far greater and firmly rooted in reason. In other words, we love because it

dominicanajournal.org/wp-content/files/old-journal-archive/vol18/no3/dominicanav18n3stthomashisteachingonfamily.pdf.

[263] See Hanna Rosin, "The End of Men," *The Atlantic*, July/August 2010, accessed May 27, 2019, https://www.theatlantic.com/magazine/archive/2010/07/the-end-ofmen/308135/. See also Glenn T. Stanton, "Are Men Necessary?," Focus on the Family, July 2, 2010, accessed May 27, 2019, https://www.focusonthefamily.com/about/focus-findings/marriage/are-men-necessary.

drives us toward what we are. We love another because of physical attraction, to be sure, but that merely is the top layer or veneer of what love really is. To love extends far beyond the physical dimension, for our physical bodies are utterly corruptible and will fade no matter what interventions are sought. Our love of others, of friends, of God, is not a physical interaction but borne of charity, that virtue of selflessness and sacrifice. In Christian parlance we often hear that "God so loved the world, as to give his only begotten Son,"[264] and that salvific act was being the sacrificial Lamb for the sins of the world.

Aristotle

In the first place there must be a union of those who cannot exist without each other; namely, of male and female, that the race may continue (and this is a union which is formed, not of deliberate purpose, but because, in common with other animals and with plants, mankind have a natural desire to leave behind them an image of themselves), and of natural ruler and subject, that both may be preserved.[265]

Aquinas

The principal end of matrimony, [is] the good of the offspring. For nature intends not only the begetting of offspring, but also its education and development until it reach the perfect state of man as man, and that is the

[264] John 3:16.
[265] *Pol.*, 1280a31.

> state of virtue. Hence ... we derive three things from our parents, namely "existence," "nourishment," and "education."[266]
>
> The secondary end of matrimony ... is the mutual services which married persons render one another in household matters. For just as natural reason dictates that men should live together [in society], ... so too among those works that are necessary for human life some are becoming to men, others to women. Wherefore nature inculcates that society of man and woman which consists in matrimony.[267]

Love is not merely a matter of sensual attraction and should never be equated with lust as its synonym. Aquinas understands that the physical dimension of love, in the attraction, the procreative sexual act, and the propagation of the species, never suffices in any true notion of love. The physical union must eventually lead to a "spiritual union" with our ultimate end and purpose for human life—God. God, being love Himself, is our natural destiny.[268] Aristotle confirms the metaphysical, transcendent nature of love when writing of "friendship" as being for the young, often "amorous" and aiming "at pleasure," which in turn causes them to "fall in love and quickly fall out of love, changing often within a single day," while those older, and in the marital state, hope "to spend their days and lives together."[269]

[266] Aquinas, *Summa*, Supp., q. 41, art. 1.
[267] Ibid.
[268] Aquinas, *Summa*, I–II, q. 62, art. 3, corp.
[269] *Nic. Ethics*, 1156a1–5.

The idea of love constitutes more than a faddish trend or personal desire, and this devaluation of love, uncoupling love from our essential nature and overall inclinations and predispositions, has had draconian consequences in a society riddled with social-familial problems. A long-term analysis of marriage data manifests a crumbling institution. Dr. Randal Olson, who tracked a century and a half of marriage statistics, charts the precipitous decline in the choice to be married.[270]

The data graph demonstrates deep and unequivocal distress in marriage, from its height of permanency and acceptability after World War II to its free fall into the twenty-first century. This same figure simultaneously portrays data on divorce for the same period, which, not surprisingly, shows an upward trek with few or minimal exceptions since 1860. No institution can survive divisive fractures at either end, that is, the act of marriage or its dissolution by divorce.

Children who suffer under these many forms of experimentation are not rocks—deadened to the emotional consequences of fatherless families, adulterous and promiscuous parents, uncommitted partners who live in open arrangements, gender bias, or confusion in parental roles, to name just a few. None of these arrangements operate in a vacuum of a distilled, calculating, and unaffected child. Our suicide rates, drug usage plague, and emotional and psychiatric difficulties so obvious to any honest observer of human life tell us everything about what this sort of chaos delivers.[271]

[270] Randal S. Olson, "144 Years of Marriage and Divorce in 1 Chart," June 15, 2015, accessed March 1, 2019, http://www.randalolson.com/2015/06/15/144-years-of-marriage-and-divorce-in-1-chart/. Visit his website for the results.

[271] Christine H. Fewell, "Attachment, Reflective Function, Family Dysfunction, and Psychological Distress among College Students

To be certain, the "novel" and unshackled family and marital state do not deliver much happiness. If happiness be a sort of ordered, contented state of being in human affairs, how does modern familial malaise do anything but deliver the opposite result? Aristotle and Aquinas cut right to the core of the modern disintegration in family life with some key reminders.

Aristotle

The family is the association established by nature for the supply of men's everyday wants.... But when several families are united, and the association aims at something more than the supply of daily needs, the first society to be formed is the village.... And therefore, if the earlier forms of society are natural, so is the state, for it is the end of them, and the nature of a thing is its end. For what each thing is when fully developed, we call its nature, whether we are speaking of a man, a horse, or a family.[272]

Aquinas

Now a child cannot be brought up and instructed unless it have certain and definite parents, and this would not be the case unless there were a tie between the man

with Alcoholic Parents," *Bridging Disciplinary Boundaries* (January 11–14, 2007), accessed May 27, 2019, https://sswr.confex.com/sswr/2007/techprogram/P7130.HTM.

[272] *Pol.*, 1280a31, 1252a26.

> and a definite woman and it is in this that matrimony consists.[273]

The Aristotelian examination of marriage and family tends to look at these communal components as part of the political and governmental order with the very basic conclusion that the health of the state or nation depends on the health of its family unit.[274] Being in a family is utterly natural; mutual attachment between husband and wife is one of the highest forms of bond and friendship, and strengthening these bonds is crucial to the survival and maintenance of a healthy community. Aristotle comments:

> The friendship between man and wife seems to be inherent in us by nature. For man is by nature more inclined to live in couples than to live as a social and political being, inasmuch as the household is earlier and more indispensable than the state, and to the extent that procreation is a bond more universal to all living things [than living in a state]. In the case of other animals, the association goes no further than this. But human beings live together not merely for procreation, but also to secure the needs of life. There is division of labor from the very beginning and different functions for man and wife. Thus they satisfy

[273] Aquinas, *Summa*, Supp., q. 41, art. 1.

[274] John Hittinger, "Plato and Aristotle on the Family and the *Polis*," *The Saint Anselm Journal* 8, no. 2 (Spring 2013), accessed May 27, 2019, https://www.anselm.edu/sites/default/files/Documents/Institute%20of%20SA%20Studies/Hittinger,%20The%20family%20and%20the%20polis.pdf.

one another's needs by contributing each his own to the common store.[275]

All around us we witness the family and its core component, the marital state, in deep, deep distress. The birth of children without two parents, once carrying a bit of social stigma, once considered outside acceptable moral norms, is now without any ethical or moral critique (see figure 6.4).[276]

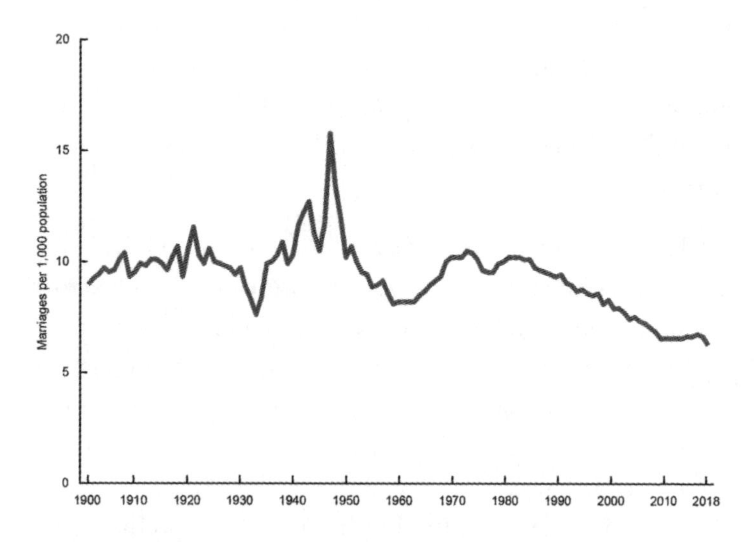

Figure 6.4. Marriage Rates: United States, 1900–2018.

[275] *Nic. Ethics*, 1162a17.

[276] Sally Curtin and Paul Sutton, *Marriage Rates in the United States, 1900–2018* (National Center for Health Statistics Health E-Stats, 2020); National Center for Health Statistics, National Vital Statistics System, Marriage, accessed January 2, 2022, at https://www.cdc.gov/nchs/data/hestat/marriage_rate_2018/Estat_fig1.png.

No one is arguing that the parent or the child be treated in negative terms, yet at the same time, to act as if this way of life has no downside or cultural impact can only be described as naïve and delusional. The rising out-of-wedlock birth rates, across all groups and ethnicities, should give even the most jaded social commentator reasons for concern (see figure 6.5).[277]

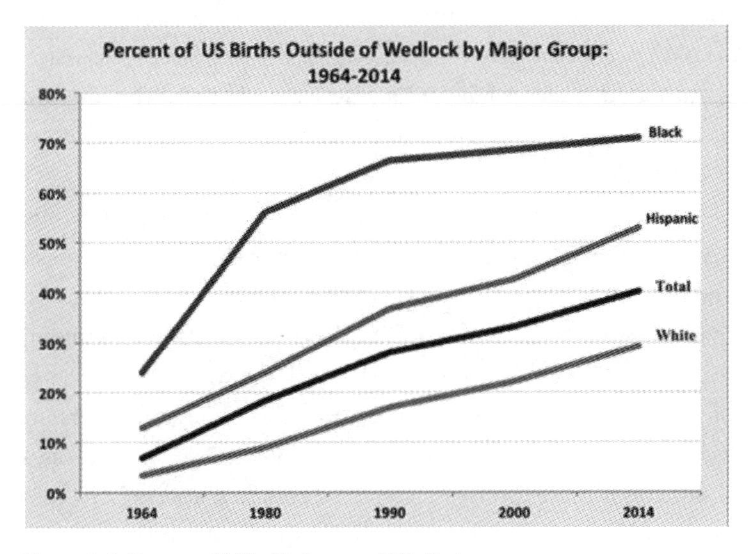

Figure 6.5. Percent of U.S. Births out of Wedlock.

And these figures are not a uniquely American experience, for across nearly every part of the civilized world, the growth in these birth statistics is aggressively high. As noted in *YaleGlobal Online*, the Organization for Economic and Co-operative Development

[277] Joseph Chamie, "Out-of-Wedlock Births Rise Worldwide," YaleGobal Online, March 16, 2017, accessed May 27, 2019, https://yale-global.yale.edu/content/out-wedlock-births-rise-worldwide.

graphs the disturbing and alarming rate of the rise of out-of-wedlock births since 1964.[278]

None of this data foretells a future of familial stability or the structure necessary for healthy and happy children. Throughout the Western world, commentators repeatedly opine on the aberrant state of violence evident in many young people, the mass shootings in schools, and the human trafficking of children for sexual purposes. Active shooters multiply at a faster pace each month, and it seems fair and just to examine the disintegration of the family and marriage as one of the most important variables (see figure 6.6).[279]

These tragedies are but a sliver of the whole problem where the devaluation of life itself, the marginalization of children as nuisances and interferers with career and ambition, and the inane conclusion that two parents are a relic of the past, if we just take a moment, will explain a good bit of it. Children kill themselves not because of phones or bullying alone but because these vulnerable persons lack the confidence and assurances that someone, somewhere, cares about and is there for them. The same commentary could be said of women who suffer abuse from tortuous boyfriends, who cannot or will not marry but instead like the arrangement where they can walk at any time and use and abuse the partner they refuse to commit to. All of this is common sense, yet our intelligentsia and elites dare not even utter such words for fear of insulting someone by imposing an objective standard for human happiness.

[278] Ibid.

[279] "Quick Look: 277 Active Shooter Incidents in the United States from 2000 to 2018," Federal Bureau of Investigation, accessed January 2, 2022, https://www.fbi.gov/about/partnerships/office-of-partner-engagement/active-shooter-incidents-graphics.

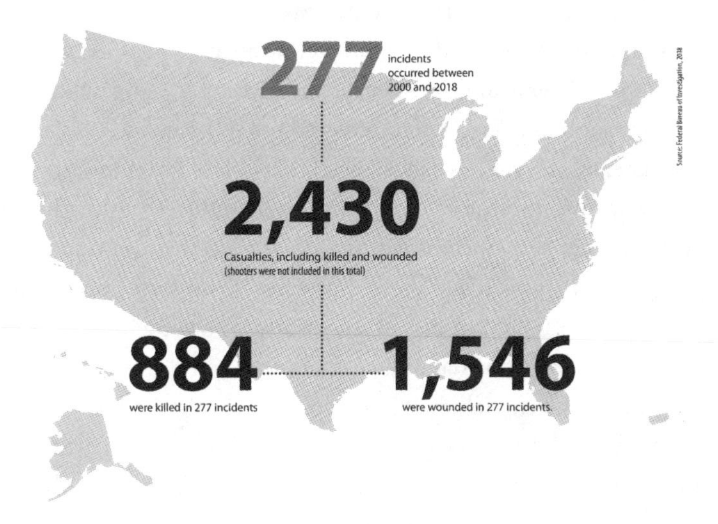

Figure 6.6. Active Shooter Incident Statistics.

Despite the compelling evidence that cohabitation before marriage is predictive of higher levels of abuse and future divorce if the parties ever marry, the social and behavioral scientists, as well as moralists and policy makers, act as if there are no consequences.[280] The research on what is termed the "cohabitation effect" cannot be glossed over as a matter of convention or preference, for the data demonstrate most of the effects over the remainder of life are less than positive.

[280] See G. H. Kline et al., "Timing Is Everything: Pre-engagement Cohabitation and Increased Risk for Poor Marital Outcomes," *Journal of Family Psychology* 18 (2004): 311–318; S. M. Stanley, G. Kline Rhoades, and H. J. Markman, "Sliding versus Deciding: Inertia and the Premarital Cohabitation Effect," *Family Relations* 55, no. 4 (2006): 499–509, accessed May 27, 2019, https://www.jstor.org/stable/40005344.

Instead of an orderly, structured society, the contemporary, chic relativist finds no difference in any arrangement of marriage and family. Everything goes because everything is going right along. Nearly every case of mass murderer, school shooter, and cultural destroyer exhibits and has experienced this lack of order in some way.

Why our empiricists comprehensively refuse to study the correlation between cultural rot, the destruction of the traditional family, and the warped view that everything is as good as any other situation should disturb us greatly. For failing to look hard and incisively at this data makes happiness a bit more difficult if not impossible to achieve. However, the empiricist has fallen so far away from reaching any moral conclusion, the subject matter likely never crosses his or her mind. For those that study the correlation, like the Heritage Foundation, the conclusion is obvious:

> The unfortunate fact that broken family relationships are often associated with greater risk factors for youths is nothing new. For decades, study after study has shown that stable, intact families play a vital role in developing thriving children and adolescents. Adolescents living in intact families are less likely to exhibit violent behaviors or engage in physical fighting, and youths in fatherless homes are significantly more likely to be incarcerated than are those from two-parent homes.[281]

What is inescapable is that stable marriages and stable family lives provide an environment with the most open and accessible path to human happiness.

[281] John Malcolm and Amy Swearer, "3 Common Traits of School Shooters," The Heritage Foundation, March 26, 2018, accessed May 27, 2019, https://www.heritage.org/education/commentary/3-common-traits-school-shooters.

In marriage itself, particularly those that last for long periods of time, the happiness between couples, while never perfect and fully absent of bickering and dispute, is a bedrock of human comfort over the long haul of those relationships.[282]

And this willful ignorance about the role and criticality of marriage in the lifeblood of any nation has enormous personal, social, and human implications, not to mention a significant impact on minimizing chances at happiness. For those laboring as single parents are more likely to be more under siege, more likely to have errant children, and more likely to suffer stresses and strains less noticeable in two-parent households. This does not imply that single parents do not labor mightily against the odds, nor does it infer that two-parent families always do a better job than the single counterpart, nor is this observation predictive in a universal sense. Even so, ask any single parent if, having their druthers, they would not prefer a partner in life to assist in the many heavy responsibilities. Single parenting, without the benefit of marriage, is undeniably a more stressful obligation than working with a good person who seeks similar ends. The National Association of Scholars summarizes the negative impacts:

> Approximately 40 percent of single-mother families are in poverty. Children born to single mothers and living without two biological parents are vastly more likely to lack parenting and early development, perform poorly in school and

[282] See William Tucker, *Marriage and Civilization: How Monogamy Made Us Human* (Washington, DC: Regnery, 2014). See also William H. Young, "Marriage and Family in Western Civilization," National Association of Scholars, September 1, 2011, accessed May 27, 2019, https://www.nas.org/articles/Marriage_and_Family_in_Western_Civilization.

drop out of high school, have behavioral and psychological problems, and themselves go on to have out-of-wedlock families. Out-of-wedlock births, now an epidemic in the lowest socioeconomic class, are a chief cause of increasing American economic inequality and the social stratification of a new underclass of the unemployable. Despite that abysmal record, college texts still exaggerate the costs of marriage to adults, particularly women, and downplay or ignore the benefits of marriage and the well-being of children.[283]

The natural preference for a family structure causes most to hope and pine for a partner, someone to share the heady responsibility of child-rearing. By no means does this analysis undercut the goodwill and efforts if parents must do it all alone, nor is there any effort to whitewash bad, dysfunctional two-parent families. Indeed, the world encounters high levels of dysfunction in the traditional family with great regularity. Even so, the challenges that arise from single parenting in nonmarital situations are significant and often studied, even though current academic circles seek to use the sheer volume of single-parent families to downplay the results. Like the explanation for changing a crime to a non-crime, the argument depends on the regularity of the action to demonstrate its acceptability. However, the data are difficult to debate.[284] The American Psychological Association lays out a list of "stressors":

[283] Young, "Marriage." Some studies indicate that the negative effects are largely overblown—for example, Dominic Schmuck, "Single Parenting: Fewer Negative Effects of Children's Behaviors Than Claimed," *Modern Psychological Studies* 18, no. 2 (2013), accessed May 27, 2019, https://scholar.utc.edu/mps/vol18/iss2/12.

[284] Sara McLanahan, "The Consequences of Single Parenthood for Subsequent Generations," accessed May 27, 2019, https://www.irp.wisc.edu/publications/focus/pdfs/foc113c.pdf.

- Visitation and custody problems
- The effects of continuing conflict between the parents
- Less opportunity for parents and children to spend time together
- Effects of the breakup on children's school performance and peer relations
- Disruptions of extended family relationships
- Problems caused by the parents' dating and entering new relationships[285]

A major university study on single motherhood and adolescent behavior manifested a "consistent association between single motherhood and increased youth psychosocial maladjustment,"[286] although more research should be undertaken to confirm its results.

When comparing levels of depression disorders and symptoms, the evidence consistently displays a higher level of depression, sadness, and maladjustment in children living in the single-parent setting (see figure 6.7).[287]

No one disputes the efforts and courage exhibited by those entrusted with single-parent responsibilities. In many ways, these stories encompass a personal courageousness and steadfastness that can only be admired. However, the lack of a partner cannot be dismissed as an annoyance or incidental triviality, for most studies of single parents do in fact demonstrate that the "general

[285] "Single Parenting and Today's Family," American Psychological Association, October 31, 2019, accessed May 27, 2019, https://www.apa.org/helpcenter/single-parent.

[286] Issar Daryanai et al., "Single Mother Parenting and Adolescent Psychopathology," *Journal of Abnormal Child Psychology* 44, no. 7 (2016): 1411–1423, accessed May 27, 2019, https://www.ncbi.nlm.nih.gov/pmc/articles/PMC5226056.

[287] Ibid.

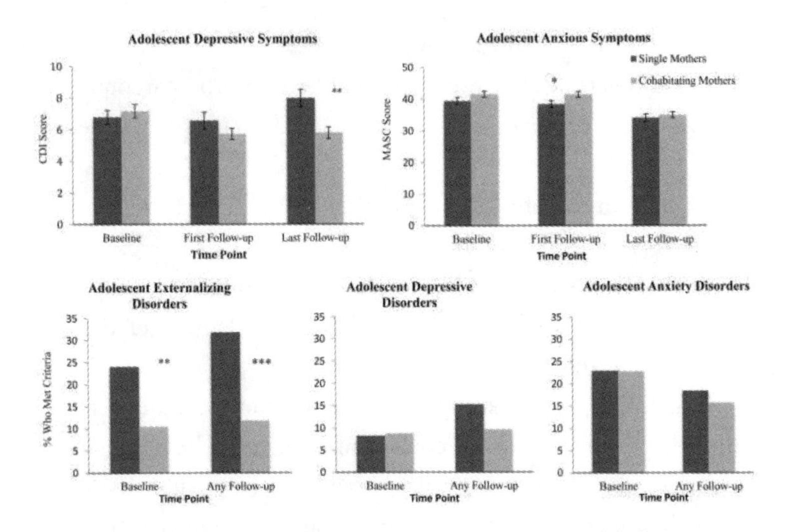

Figure 6.7. Teenage Depression Rates.

level of happiness among unmarried women is lower than among their married counterparts."[288]

All of this analysis paints a troubled picture of a society under familial and marital pressures, and those pressures become very particularized for both the single parent and the children inhabiting this brave, new, and very isolated way of parental oversight. For it is not just the parent who experiences this isolation but the children who by nature look to parents, in the plural sense of the word. Children are not sophisticated enough, as are the moral elites, to rationalize and justify the terms and conditions of their family existence. The innocence of children should rightly assume a mother

[288] Anna Baranowska-Rataj, Anna Matysiak, and Monika Mynarska, "Does Lone Motherhood Decrease Women's Happiness? Evidence from Qualitative and Quantitative Research," *Journal of Happiness Studies* 15, no. 6 (December 2014): 1457.

and a father, one who maternally gives birth in the exclusive role as mother and one who cares and provides as a father for both mother and children during this time of family development. No particular formula is self-evident, and marriage does not preclude two careers, two incomes, or the decision of a father remaining home to care for children or a mother being the primary breadwinner. All of these issues are fully negotiable. The issue here is the partnership and the joint effort to provide a familial environment where the child knows both figures, rather than just one.

The dramatic rise of children living in a single-parent household should not be dismissed as some insignificant computation on the state of the American family but instead should be recognized as a warning bell calling for a bit more assessment on how this impacts the culture and the collective (see figure 6.8).[289]

In the final analysis, the relationship between marriage and happiness appears more probative than not. Marriage does many, many things to the participants, both good and bad, although most of its effects are positive. On balance, aside from the structural integrity it provides husbands, wives, and children, marriage provides boundaries, parameters, and fencing, so to speak, in a world that is often fenceless. Marriage gives context to procreation, to love and charity, to sexuality and propagation of the species, and most importantly, marriage engenders some of our greatest virtues. Loyalty to one another, kindness, selflessness and unbounded charity, sacrifice and caring, and fidelity and the bond of our promises,

[289] Paul Hemez and Chanell Washington, "Number of Children Living Only with Their Mothers Has Doubled in Past 50 Years," United States Census Bureau, April 12, 2021, accessed January 2, 2022, https://www.census.gov/library/stories/2021/04/number-of-children-living-only-with-their-mothers-has-doubled-in-past-50-years.html.

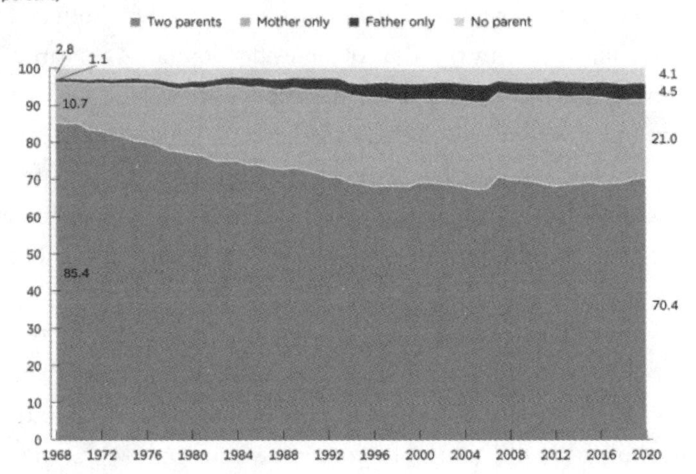

Figure 6.8. Living Arrangements of Children under Eighteen, 1968–2020.

to name just a few virtuous dispositions, make marriage the most cogent way any civilization can depend on a strong and moral citizenry. Because marriage naturally and structurally requires virtue, and its success depends upon a virtuous and caring disposition, happiness is more likely to flourish than not.[290]

A recent study from the University of Vancouver and the National Bureau of Economic Research compared and contrasted, over a long period of time, the correlation between life satisfaction, or happiness as can be substituted, and marriage. The results

[290] See Tony Vinson and Matthew Ericson, "The Social Dimensions of Happiness and Life Satisfaction of Australians: Evidence from the World Values Survey," *International Journal of Social Welfare* 23, no. 3 (July 2014): 240–253, accessed May 27, 2019, https://doi.org/10.1111/ijsw.12062.

clearly indicate higher rates for the married state when compared to no marital history.[291]

Marriage also provides a relational setting rather than an isolated corner of human interaction, and this relational quality of marriage becomes more and more important as the years pass and old age sets in. Social relationships of every sort tend to foster "very happy people"[292] when compared to a life of lonely isolation. On the other hand, a conflicted and turbulent marriage, built of rancor and deceit, will not only hinder happiness but also produce higher levels of "physical disability and depressed effect."[293] In the more contented and conflict-free marriages, the results are happily positive, with health and psychological outlooks and states strikingly better than relationships built on marital dysfunction. Marriage delivers the relational setting for personal contentment and an inherent "social connectedness" that far surpasses social isolation.[294]

In *Nicomachean Ethics*, Aristotle notes that marriage is "rooted" in "a natural complementarity between man and woman." This "natural complementarity" results in "friendship." In book 8, chapter 7 of *Nicomachean Ethics*, Aristotle explains that although

[291] See Shawn Grover and John F. Helliwell, "How's Life at Home? New Evidence on Marriage and the Set Point for Happiness," "National Bureau of Economic Research Working Paper 20794" (Cambridge, MA, December 2014), accessed May 27, 2019, https://www.nber.org/papers/w20794.pdf.

[292] Robert J. Waldinger and Marc S. Schulz, "What's Love Got to Do with It?: Social Functioning, Perceived Health, and Daily Happiness in Married Octogenarians," *Psychology of Aging* 25, no. 2 (2010): 424.

[293] Ibid., 424.

[294] Ibid., 425.

the relationship of husband and wife is one of "superiority," it is still possible for a husband and wife to be friends.[295]

Aquinas

A joining denotes a kind of uniting, and so wherever things are united there must be a joining. Now things directed to one purpose are said to be united in their direction thereto, thus many men are united in following one military calling or in pursuing one business, in relation to which they are called fellow-soldiers or business partners. Hence, since by marriage certain persons are directed to one begetting and upbringing of children, and again to one family life, it is clear that in matrimony there is a joining in respect of which we speak of husband and wife; and this joining, through being directed to some one thing, is matrimony; while the joining together of bodies and minds is a result of matrimony.[296]

Of course, many of these observations will depend upon quality-of-life determinations and levels of economic prosperity too, for it takes more than just a long-term marriage to be happy. The better observation might be that healthy and self-sufficient marital partners tend be happier and filled with greater well-being than the unhealthy and economically challenged marital partner. Common

[295] *Nic. Ethics*, 1158b14–30, 1158b25, 1158b30–35. See Vallerie Marie Stein, "Husband and Wife in Aristotle's Politics" (master's thesis, Boston College, 2016), accessed May 27, 2019, https://dlib.bc.edu/islandora/object/bc-ir:107143/datastream/PDF/view.

[296] Aquinas, *Summa*, Supp., q. 44, corp.

sense dictates that happiness comes to rely on many forces for either its increase or diminishment. Research, however, shows that the marital state is more likely than not to help ward off health problems and provide a support system to reconcile and live with these challenges a bit better. Data from the English Longitudinal Study of Ageing and the U.S. Health and Retirement Study, gathered during 2006 to 2008 and just published in 2019, paint a fascinating picture of how these variables interweave and interlock.[297] In sum, the study indicates that "research shows that those that are married have better physical and psychological health and greater longevity than their unmarried counterparts, as well as better health than those are in unmarried cohabitating relationships."[298]

In this finding, the advantage marriage brings to both of its participants, the offspring resulting from this conjugal union, and the collective that counts happy people among its members, cannot be summarily discounted. For in this small setting exists a flourishing rooted in love and virtue, sacrifice and selflessness, which in turn are a nation-state's finest building blocks.

Happiness, Family, and Children

Aristotle

Human beings live together not only for the sake of reproduction but also for the various purposes of life;

[297] Natasha Wood et al., "Marriage and Physical Capability at Mid to Later Life in England and the USA," *PLoS ONE* 14, no. 1 (January 23, 2019), accessed May 27, 2019, https://doi.org/10.1371/journal.pone.0209388.

[298] Ibid.

> from the start the functions are divided, and those of man and woman are different; so they help each other by throwing their particular gifts into the common stock.... For each has its own excellence and they will delight in the fact. And children seem to be a good of union (which is why childless people part more easily); for children are a good common to both and what is common holds them together.[299]

Aquinas

> Now a child cannot be brought up and instructed unless it have certain and definite parents, and this would not be the case unless there were a tie between the man and a definite woman, and it is in this that matrimony consists.... Wherefore nature inculcates that society of man and woman which consists in matrimony.[300]

Aristotle and Aquinas do not leave their analysis of marriage and family without a full consideration of the role and purpose of children in this sacred institution. Children, that is, offspring, are the natural, associative gift in marriage, for they are part of the inevitable bond and glue that cements the marital state. In the case of Aquinas, the begetting and procreation of children arises from our own natural inclinations to procreate and propagate the species. It is an inherent tenet of our own natural law, something evident throughout human history and cultural evaluation. Without natural propagation, the species would end.

[299] *Nic. Ethics*, 1162a15–30.

[300] Aquinas, *Summa*, Supp., q. 41, art. 1, corp.

And because of this natural inclination, being part of the natural law, which reflects the eternal law of God, having children is part of our natural makeup. Terms like *biological clock* and the rise of fertility clinics edify this predisposition to have children. Even those who are in non-heterosexual relationships eventually weigh the decision on children. It is hard to avoid what we are naturally predisposed to. And while many people go long periods without thinking much about children, inevitably, as time passes and the parties age, there is a pull, so to speak, to have children—a natural biological urge that appears common to *Homo sapiens*. This biological tug is not the sole reason people have children, for there are a host of other reasons such as the strengthening of the bond of marriage, sacrifice and selflessness, extending the boundaries of human interaction and affection, assuring a legacy, and developing strong citizens for the common good and the collective. While nature surely drives a large portion of reproduction and procreation, emotions are at play here. For over time, marriage, by its very nature, hopes to expand its loving influence to others and, by the natural attraction and affection of husband and wife, to generate children as a manifestation of that human sexuality. None of these observations are new and all are fully understood in the pagan world of Aristotle and the very Catholic world of Aquinas.[301]

Having children may be the natural instinct for propagation, but this drive or impulse alone is simply insufficient. Having children reflects the union of people in marriage, the unity of joining with one another on many levels, including the act of physical, sexual

[301] See John Witte Jr., "The Goods and Goals of Marriage," *Notre Dame Law Review* 76, no. 3 (2001): 1019–1071, accessed May 27, 2019, https://scholarship.law.nd.edu/cgi/viewcontent.cgi?article=1557&context=ndlr.

intercourse, an act Aquinas holds is never a "sin" in the marital state and often, and properly so, governed by the "intensity of pleasure" natural to the sexual act in the marital state.[302]

If we accept these views on children as true, it is fair to discern a natural and evident correlation between happiness and children or, in the reverse, an unhappiness that might result from never having children. No one claims this is an easy question to resolve, for many people choose to have no children; others, for medical or biological reasons, are precluded from bearing children, and some, such as priests and nuns, elect to lead celibate lives, a decision that separates them from the possibility of having children. And some people live the single life in a purposeful way, because that seems their destiny or because circumstances and events did not coalesce to ensure marriage.

None of this is so cut and dry to apply a universal, standardized test of propriety in regard to children. However, the mass and bulk of humanity, given the billions and billions of births quite apparent throughout human history, appear to be driven toward a procreative life. This too seems more than a matter of convention, like lemmings following other lemmings off a cliff, but instead an inclination that generates certain rewards that make a life without children impossible to imagine. The joy of children and the many frustrations common to the nurturing process make having children both demanding and, at the same time, fulfilling. Happiness and unhappiness often sit side by side in the question of having and raising children, and even helping them act properly. In the eyes of Aristotle and Aquinas, for marriage to reach its full flourishing and the proper ends the institution serves, children need to be part of that equation.

[302] Aquinas, *Summa*, Supp., q. 41, art. 1, ad 6.

Aristotle

Between man and wife friendship seems to exist by nature; for man is naturally inclined to form couples, even more than to form cities, inasmuch as the household is earlier and more necessary than the city and reproduction is more common to man with the animals.[303]

Aquinas

In man, however, since the child needs the parents' care for a long time, there is a very great tie between male and female, to which tie even the generic nature inclines.[304]

Stated in Aristotelian terms, marriage cannot reach its full "potentiality" without children, and in Thomistic terms, marriage must be about the "begetting and upbringing of children, and again to one family life."[305] The alternatives to this conclusion drive toward natural extinction, for without the propagation of the species, our commentary becomes not only moot but nihilistic. In many ways, in the age of controlled and artificial reproduction, with abortion now posed as a fourth-trimester right, the decriminalization of infanticide, the selective genetic shopping for traits and attributes in proposed children, and the general lack of charity and self-sacrifice in a material world, the stresses on children have never been more acute. Birth rate data continue a long-term and very precipitous decline. Similar results are reached when evaluating the fertility

[303] *Nic. Ethics*, 1162a16–28.

[304] Aquinas, *Summa*, Supp., q. 41, art. 1, ad 1.

[305] Aquinas, *Summa*, Supp., q. 44, art. 1, corp.

numbers in births per woman over a recent ten-year period as announced by the Heritage Foundation (see figure 6.9).[306]

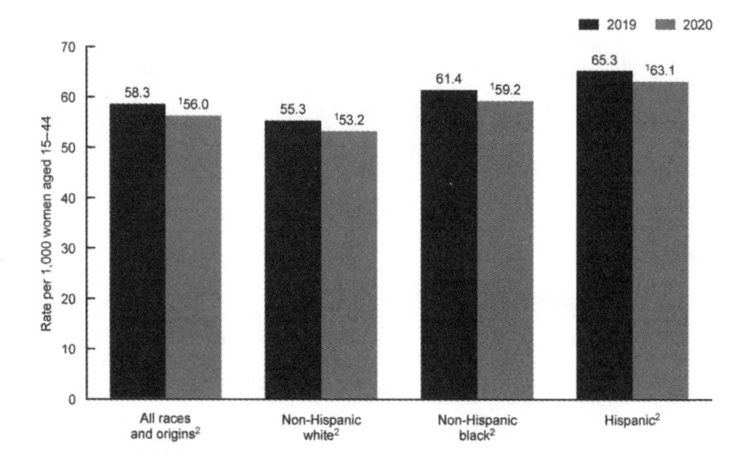

Figure 6.9. Fertility Rates.

None of these results are a uniquely American experience, with European countries now largely descending into a zero or even negative birth rate. The implications for the social and economic order of these countries can only be described as staggering and will in time produce some very unhappy results. Who shall take care of the old and the elderly if there be no young? What of labor and the natural shortages resulting from no births? What of schools, churches, and institutions that lack people to populate? What happens to a nation-state, its culture and identity when

[306] Joyce Martin, Brady Hamilton, and Michelle Osterman, *Births in the United States, 2020*, NCHS Data Brief 418 (Hyattsville, MD: National Center for Health Statistics, 2021), figure 1, accessed January 2, 2022, at https://www.cdc.gov/nchs/products/databriefs/db418.htm.

its population dissipates? None of the queries produce the type of collective happiness or individual happiness that comes from a well-organized and properly functioning political system. The Romans and Greeks, from Aristotle to Cicero, were keenly attuned to this connection between strong, healthy families and strong, healthy republics. The world birth rate, outside of third world and developing countries, has dropped in the direction of natural extinction.[307]

With so many relationships engaged in child avoidance, the question then becomes how happy and contented are these childless settings and how emotionally satisfied are these countries that have chosen their own slow elimination? Outside some extenuating circumstance or a medical issue, the bulk of childless situations frequently feature self-serving, self-aggrandizing parties who, instead of giving to others as parents or as committed couples, rest their chief intent on materialism and the amassing of goods. And yes, we have gone down a new road coupling climate change and the avoidance of children, as recently espoused by the nation's socialist celebrity—Alexandria Ocasio-Cortez.

For the state to exhort childlessness, in the name of climate change, is no different than the Maoist Chinese population edict of the "one-child family" or other tyrannical edicts from a totalitarian setting. The logic of it can only be described as befuddling, for here the state, relying upon questionable science, demands its citizens not reproduce or bear children. Even this is an absurd sideshow; it is all part of an increasing culture that finds children the ultimate nuisance and barrier to money, to fame, to career and job, to convenience and freedom, to privacy and mental health. Despite the

[307] Visit the CIA World Factbook at https://www.indexmundi.com/g/r.aspx?v=25 for the statistics.

correlations between children and happiness, the modern mantra about children is very much against children. Michael Murray's classic moral text, *Problems in Conduct*, appreciates the symbiotic and compellingly emotional bond that exists between children and their parents, and this deep affection cannot be summarily dismissed or controlled. He notes,

> The duty of caring for the child belongs to both parents because both are the causes of the child's existence. This duty is satisfied only when the offspring is physically, intellectually, and morally capable of proper human living. Naturally, mother and father, woman and man, have different physical and psychological capacities that are mutually complementary, and the influence of both parties is required for the proper development of the child.[308]

Accepting this natural responsibility and the natural inclinations to procreate, and to care for, educate, and nurture our offspring, efforts to the contrary will likely lead to less happiness. For if anything has come across throughout this text, it is the conclusion that acting in accordance with nature will produce a more beneficial and positive result for the human actor than acting in contravention to that nature.[309]

Most academic literature tends to support the broad assertion above, for children bring, as already noted, a further intimacy and

[308] Michael V. Murray, *Problems in Conduct* (New York: Holt, Rinehart, and Winston, 1963), 226.

[309] There are those who argue otherwise. See Kei M. Nomaguchi and Melissa A. Milkie, "Costs and Rewards of Children: The Effects of Becoming a Parent on Adults' Lives," *Journal of Marriage and Family* 65, no. 2 (May 2003): 356–374.

bonding to relationships that would not exist otherwise. Some call it "life satisfaction" and others a true "meaning in life."[310]

Children bring many elements to the table in a marriage, not all of which are particularly memorable, especially when one considers sleeplessness, additional financial costs, less personal autonomy, and even time for husbands and wives. To be sure, these descriptors take up the nuisance side of childbearing and child-rearing. Contrast these inconveniences with the grander benefits of having children, and the former stresses may be just a little less important. For studies show that children cause parents to see the world in very different terms than previously. A few more memorable benefits include but are not limited to:

- Finding purpose in life
- Discovering meaning for life and the marital relationship
- Generation of positive emotions
- Enhanced maternal and paternal roles
- Caring for others by sacrifice[311]

In a sense, children, when viewed through the prism of charity and the natural order, are not only a blessing but a challenge worth engaging. As one scholar on the family commented, "Children are the fount of our greatest joys and the source of our greatest sorrows ... blissful and gratifying ... stressful and

[310] See S. Katherine Nelson et al., "In Defense of Parenthood: Children Are Associated with More Joy than Misery," *Psychological Science* 24, no. 1 (2013): 3–10. See also Luis Angeles, "Children and Life Satisfaction," *Journal of Happiness Studies* 11, no. 4 (August 2010): 523–538.

[311] S. Katherine Nelson, Kostadin Kushlev, and Sonja Lyubomirsky, "The Pains and Pleasures of Parenting: When, Why, and How Is Parenthood Associated with More or Less Well-Being?," *Psychological Bulletin* 140, no. 3 (2014): 846–895.

challenging."[312] What is clear from many studies is that parents with children tend to be happier than those without the blessings of offspring. Instead of seeing these obligations as shackles to be unleashed, many parents find joy in the responsibility of raising their children, deriving more "positive feeling from caring for their children than from other daily activities."[313] In general, many studies have demonstrated that "parents are happier overall compared to nonparents."[314]

Of course, many of these observations do not consider extraordinary circumstances such as heavy economic pressure from a loss of job, mental or physical challenges for the children, or abusive settings for mothers trying to raise children. Whether or not a parent is happy is not dictated by the biological offspring variable alone but by a host of other criteria that measure the quality and condition of life. And whether or not that marital situation remains intact is another critical variable affecting the happiness question, for single parents, by and large, must labor under more difficult conditions than functioning dual parents. The import of a stable marriage cannot be overstated since "most unmarried individuals appear to be worse off with children."[315]

One other variable that impacts overall happiness in marriage with regard to children relates to the age of those children: most parents experience less emotional stress with young infant children and far more with developing adolescent children. This finding should not surprise anyone with teenage children, and even adult children, where the stresses and strains of modern life often lead

[312] Ibid., 846.
[313] Nelson, "Defense," 3.
[314] Ibid., 4.
[315] Angeles, "Children," 523.

to complex and difficult rearing issues. Hence, happiness levels may drop off a little as children mature into adults—but this is a natural reality of the eventual separation of children from the very parents that loved and nurtured them.[316]

Conclusion

While the analysis in these pages can never be equated with any sort of perfect science or mathematical precision, it appears that there is a strong correlation between achieving happiness and marriage, family, and children. Nearly all academic studies indicate that trouble emerges for those born into dysfunctional and troublesome families. The literature also makes plain that the formal institution of marriage, on a fast and precipitous decline, is an essential building block for any functioning society and its members, and a sort of parameter or guide for its citizenry. Strong families and strong marriages lead to strong children and strong communities. One cannot sever the association.

Every other form of association or relationship lacks the stability and permanency that marriage and matrimony provide the family structure. By contrast, Hollywood stars that shun marriage for its convention and traditional moorings live inescapably miserable lives characterized by multiple relationships and slavish addictions. Children chicly born out of wedlock shall struggle mightily when compared to the marital offspring—in economic and emotional terms as well as the health of their future relationships. The

[316] Ann Meier et al., "Mothers' and Fathers' Well-Being in Parenting across the Arch of Child Development," *Journal of Marriage and Family* 80, no. 4 (August 2018): 992–1004, accessed May 27, 2019, https://doi.org/10.1111/jomf.12491.

cohabiting crowd that test-drives future marriages is destined to experience divorce and personal dysfunction at strikingly higher rates. In addition, cohabitation tends to foster higher rates of abuse, both physically and sexually, and the rise has been correlated to cohabitation's lack of commitment. Rates of abuse, both physical and sexual, skyrocket within these promiscuous, temporary, and informal relationships. In all of these settings, happiness is in very short supply.

Aristotle and Aquinas will also properly conclude that marriage has a naturally inclined procreative component—being open to intimacy that is always open to new life. The affection and love expressed by the physical joining of a husband and wife is incapable of reaching fruition in the world of artificial birth control, abortion, and infanticide, nor will these controls comport with living in accordance with our natural inclinations and functions. To be joined, to enter into physical union within a marriage, is to be open to the procreative act. No civilization can survive a birth and child policy of oppressive and controlled family size. Efforts to control family size are totally contrary to the law of nature and the natural law. Acting in contravention to nature never produces as meaningful a happiness state as acting in consort with nature. Hence, to choose conduct in accordance with our natural dispositions is to not only materially and physically join in the bonds of matrimony but also to engage in a "spiritual joining together."[317]

From these observations it is a fair conclusion to hold that happiness comes more readily both to those who commit to marriage, in the formal and even sacramental sense, and to those less resistant to the procreative end and purpose of the conjugal and sexual union. If we simply examine the sexual act without

[317] Aquinas, *Summa*, Supp., q. 45, art. 1, corp.

purposeful restrictions, such as birth control, then we encounter a sexual freedom that is both open to procreation and, at the same time, unworried about any consequences that the actor wishes to control. In this way, the married party, who engages in sexual intercourse with a spouse, fears nothing while on the other hand, the unmarried party, the cohabiting party—the uncommitted party—fears everything and must control it. As a result, one acts with greater autonomy, personal freedom, and integrity than the other, and that same party is likely less concerned or stressed out about implications they wish to control and check. This is precisely what St. John Paul II meant when he typed sexual promiscuity as a form of enslaved state lacking all freedom, while the marital state represents true freedom because the marital love is open to all God's gifts.[318]

The Pontifical Council for the Family states in part:

> The revealing sign of authentic married love is openness to life: "In its most profound reality, love is essentially a gift; and conjugal love ... [which] does not end with the couple, because it makes them capable of the greatest possible gift, the gift by which they become cooperators with God for giving life to a new human person. Thus the couple, while giving themselves to one another, give not just themselves but also the reality of children, who are a living reflection of their love, a permanent sign of conjugal unity and a living and inseparable synthesis of their being a father and a mother." From this communion of love and life spouses draw that human and spiritual richness and that positive

[318] See Karol Wojtyla, *Love and Responsibility* (San Francisco: Ignatius Press, 1993).

atmosphere for offering their children the support of education for love and chastity.[319]

Finally, the question of whether intentional childlessness in the marital or other state of cohabitation provides for a happier result was considered. In most academic studies, the life satisfaction rates and sense of purpose appear higher in those who have children, although the stresses and strains of being unmarried and a single parent raising children appear far higher and more keenly felt than those in the traditional dual-parent family. Anyone who would argue, despite all of the good intentions and good work of single parents, that this state be preferable to a happy marriage jointly caring for and raising children appears not to have spoken with those doing the task singularly. Child-rearing is a most challenging responsibility, and the happier place is usually the two-parent setting. In short, happiness belongs, in greater quotient, to the married person who desires and wishes for children and then welcomes offspring as a blessing, rather than to those who seek to remain unmarried, are hesitant toward procreation, and see children, if unexpectedly born, as a misery rather than a gift.

Rules for a Happy Life

6.0: That Happiness Does Not Reside in Isolation from Others

6.1: That Happiness Is Discovered in a Social, Communal Framework

[319] Pontifical Council for the Family, "The Truth and Meaning of Human Sexuality: Guidelines for Education within the Family," December 8, 1995, https://www.vatican.va/roman_curia/pontifical_councils/family/documents/rc_pc_family_doc_08121995_human-sexuality_en.html, 15.

6.2: That Happiness and Loneliness Are Antagonistic to One Another

6.3: That Happiness without Friendship Is Impossible

6.4: That Happiness Requires Giving to Others—Whether in Family, Profession, or Religious Life

6.5: That Happiness at the Individual and Communal Level Depends upon Family

6.6: That Happiness Cultivated within the Traditional Family Is the Best Design for Its Participants

6.7: That Happiness Differs in Dysfunctional or Alternative Families

6.8: That Happiness for Children Correlates to a Mother and a Father

6.9: That Happiness and the Marital State/Matrimony Are Superior to Mere Cohabitation

6.10: That Happiness in the Future Is Often Falsely Guided by Cohabitation Decisions

6.11: That Happiness in Marriage Is Fostered by the Having of Children and Being Open to the Procreative Process

6.12: That Happiness in the Marital State Is Not Negatively Impacted by Children but Blessed by Them

6.13: That Happiness Is Negatively Impacted by Efforts to Control the Birth of Children

6.14: That Happiness and Communal Health Depend upon a Strong Family Unit

7

Happiness, Spiritual Belief, and Religion

Introduction

Aristotle

Therefore the first heavens must be eternal. There is therefore also something which moves them. And since that which is moved and moves is intermediate, there is a mover which moves without being moved, being eternal, substance, and actuality.[320]

Aquinas

Final and perfect happiness can consist in nothing else than the vision of the Divine Essence. To make this clear, two points must be observed. First, that man is not perfectly happy, so long as something remains for him to desire and seek: secondly, that the perfection of any power is determined by the nature of its object....

320 Aristotle, *Metaphysics*, 1072a20–26.

> Consequently, for perfect happiness the intellect needs to reach the very Essence of the First Cause. And thus it will have its perfection through union with God as with that object, in which alone man's happiness consists.[321]

The connection between having a spiritual life, a faith rooted in theological dimensions, and happiness has long been studied.[322] Whatever the culture or religious denomination, research shows that any chance of happiness increases among those with faith and decreases among those without it. For those believing in a transcendency, something metaphysically beyond the here and the now, there is an inherent optimism that human operations and human life alone cannot provide. If one lives long enough in the temporal sphere, one is bound to be disappointed, for human beings lack any perfection—a condition reserved for a higher order. To believe in the here and now alone leads to a sort of natural desperation, a futility of purpose, for our inevitable end is not something grander, more perfect, or more meaningful, but corruption of our body alone—turning into the dust we originated from. Nothing you do here ensures eternal happiness since we are but visitors whose bodies surely die. To make any difference for the long haul of our existence beyond the body, our attention must turn to the soul because of its immortality.

[321] Aquinas, *Summa*, I–II, q. 3, art. 8, corp.

[322] For a systematic review of nearly five hundred different studies on the relationship, see Byron R. Johnson, *Objective Hope: Assessing the Effectiveness of Faith-Based Organizations: A Review of the Literature* (Waco, TX: Baylor Institute for Studies of Religion, 2008), accessed May 27, 2019, https://www.baylor.edu/content/services/document.php/24809.pdf.

For those that believe, that have faith and accept the afterlife, the results relative to depression, age span, suicide, substance abuse, and aberrant sexual behavior are stunningly better for the believers over the nonbelievers. Belief resides in the incorporeal part of the human species, not in its physical reality. A believer believes not because of a toe or an arm, a leg or a finger, but precisely because of the intangible dimension of the human person—in the mind, the soul, and the intellect. Figure 7.1[323] charts hundreds of distinct studies, covering more than 125,000 persons, that prove the positive nexus between religion and a happy life.[324]

At every criterion noted, the believer scores more favorably than the nonbeliever, in every category and in every measure. The overwhelming bulk of research on the topic shows similar results.[325]

If there is nothing beyond our own physical experiences, and nothing existing above the earthly plane, there clearly is no need for moral standards for human behavior nor would there be any

[323] Ibid., 11.

[324] Agnieszka Bozek, Pawel F. Nowak, and Mateusz Blukacz, "The Relationship between Spirituality, Health-Related Behavior, and Psychological Well-Being," *Frontiers in Psychology* 11 (August 2020), accessed January 2, 2022, at https://www.frontiersin.org/articles/10.3389/fpsyg.2020.01997/full.

[325] See ibid. See also Philip Moeller, "Why Religion Is Linked with Better Health and Well-Being," *Huff Post Wellbeing,* April 15, 2012; Matthew E. Ryan, and Andrew J. P. Francis, "Locus of Control Beliefs Mediate the Relationship between Religious Functioning and Psychological Health," *Journal of Religion and Health* 51 (2012): 774–785; R. David Hayward et al., "Externalizing Religious Health Beliefs and Health and Well-Being Outcomes," *Journal of Behavioral Medicine* 39 (2016): 887–895; Mohammed Zakir Hossain and Mohd Ahsan Kabir Rizvi, "Relationship between Religious Belief and Happiness in Oman: A Statistical Analysis," *Mental Health, Religion, and Culture* 19, no. 7 (2016): 781–790.

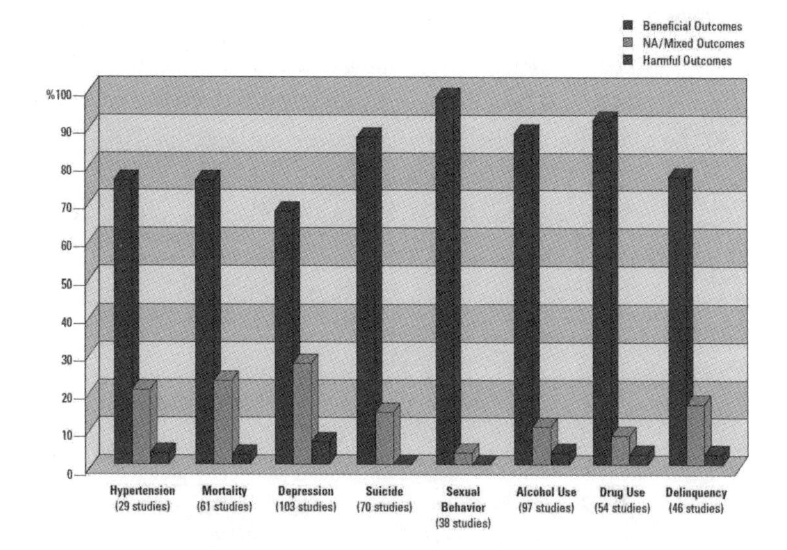

Figure 7.1. Relationship between Religion and Health Outcomes.

need to live the good life nor would it matter if we flourished or not or met our full potentiality. Excessive drinking, carousing, drug abuse and errant living would simply be conduct among a series of choices and preferences for condemnation or moral scrutiny would lack any objective basis for measure. And the nonbeliever also lacks the depth and breadth of well-being that is so far advanced in the believer; the idea that it makes sense to hope for tomorrow; the impetus for self-improvement and educational excellence; and the securing of our sense of self-worth and self-esteem. See figure 7.2.[326]

The godless state cannot provide that level of personal value nor instill any long-term confidence in its members, for the state is the likeliest of temporal, changeable, and fleeting institutions. Something much higher in the scheme of being lays out a path to

[326] Johnson, *Objective*, 14.

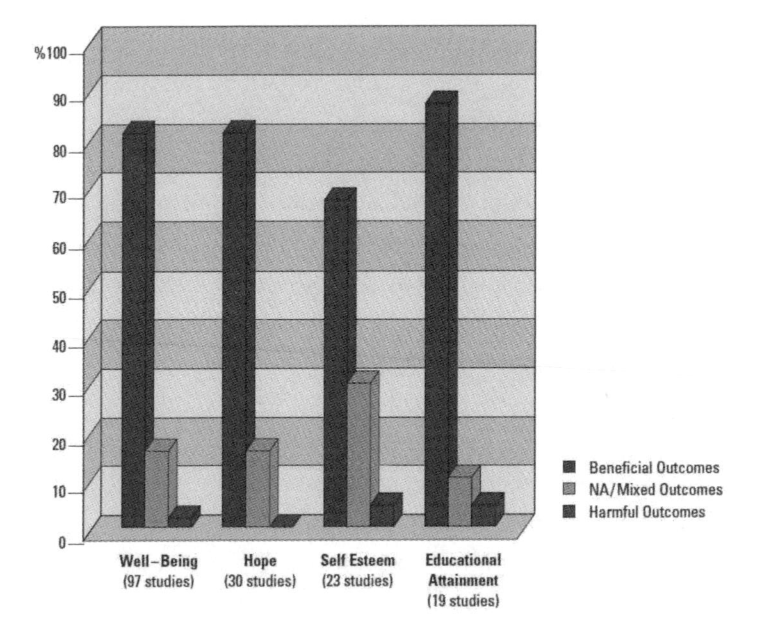

Figure 7.2. Religion and Well-Being.

personal worth and dignity, and that higher dimension is provided by a spiritual recognition and acceptance of the dimension above and beyond our little orb. Religion, faith, and the spiritual side of our being lead to extraordinary levels of happiness when compared to the bleak humanist who wants to be nice because it is nice to be nice. No cute and trite mottos, bulletin boards, banners, or posters hanging in our schools, by way of illustration, can ever replace the most fundamental reason why we must love and care for our neighbor. Saccharine slogans like Respect Self—Respect Others, while well-meaning, cannot push any party to the underlying reason human charity is so essential to the good life.

Coursing through this text has been a continual refrain, both incessantly and rightfully posed by Aristotle and Aquinas, on the goods we should seek and ends we ought to aim for. For the non-believer, the end comes as the coffin is lowered into the ground. Those who believe in a higher power accept the frailty of temporal life yet gaze at the heavens seeing a far better home. For the believer, there is something richer and more substantive than simple human activity. Even human mortality rates are directly impacted by belief or nonbelief, with a marked advantage for the longer life going toward the believer. The "level of religiousness," as one commentator put it, "has a deep impact on the level of inner content feeling in a person."[327]

In the works and thought of Aristotle, God is indispensable, for He is the logical endgame of being as told by Aristotle,[328] and our perfect happiness, according to Aquinas, can only be achieved in the presence and Beatific Vision of God.[329] Happiness remains a complete impossibility when lacking a connection to God. The God we speak of, in the case of Aristotle and Aquinas, is completely nondenominational and more aptly described as a perfect, omnipotent, omniscient being in pure actuality—nothing lacking, nothing needed. The rest of existence suffers from its natural imperfection since we are not God, nor can we ever be God or the

[327] Hossain and Rizbi, "Relationship," 782; Mohd Ahsan Kabir Rizvi and Mohammed Zakir Hossain, "Relationship between Religious Belief and Happiness: A Systematic Literature Review," *Journal of Religion and Health* 56, no. 5 (2016): 1–22.

[328] Aristotle, *Metaphysics*, 1072b25–30.

[329] See "Thomas Aquinas," Pursuit of Happiness, accessed May 27, 2019, https://www.pursuit-of-happiness.org/history-of-happiness/thomas-aquinas/. See also Joseph Stenberg, "Aquinas on the Relationship between the Vision and Delight in Perfect Happiness," *American Catholic Philosophical Quarterly* 90, no. 4 (2016): 665–680, accessed May 27, 2019, https://www.pdcnet.org/acpq/content/acpq_2016_0999_9_14_99.

gods. Throughout our lives we have yearned for and sought out God, for we know this is the home we were made for. Aristotle beautifully described the fullness and perfection of God.

Aristotle

If, then, God is always in that good state in which we sometimes are, this compels our wonder; and if in a better this compels it yet more. And God is in a better state. And life also belongs to God, for actuality is life most good and eternal. We say therefore that God is a living being, eternal, most good, so that life and duration continuous and eternal belong to God, for this is God.[330]

Aquinas

To be good belongs pre-eminently to God. For a thing is good according to its desirableness. Now everything seeks after its own perfection; and the perfection and form of an effect consist in a certain likeness to the agent, since every agent makes its like; and hence the agent itself is desirable and has the nature of good. For the very thing which is desirable in it is the participation of its likeness. Therefore, since God is the first effective cause of all things, it is manifest that the aspect of good and of desirableness belong to Him.[331]

[330] Aristotle, *Metaphysics*, 1072b25–30.

[331] Aquinas, *Summa*, I–II, q. 6, art. 1, corp.

Happiness, Physical Well-Being, Health, and the Spiritual Life

While there are a host of variables that measure the relationship between faith, belief, and a spiritual life, none illuminate the positive outcomes for this relationship more than physical health and longevity.[332] Even without empirical data, human observation alone seems to indicate longer and healthier lives for certain occupations and individuals in a formal religious life. One of the most famous studies regarding religious life, involving 678 nuns over multiple decades, is commonly labeled the "Nun Study."[333] Members of the School Sisters of Notre Dame, these nuns consented to a

[332] Stephen Rossetti, *Why Priests Are Happy: A Study of the Psychological and Spiritual Health of Priests* (Notre Dame, IN: Ave Maria Press, 2011); Leslie J. Francis and Giuseppe Crea, "Work-Related Psychological Health and Psychological Type: A Study among Catholic Priests in Italy," *Mental Health, Religion, and Culture* 18, no. 7 (2015): 593–604; Leslie J. Francis, "Happiness Is a Thing Called Stable Extraversion: A Further Examination of the Relationship between the Oxford Happiness Inventory and Eysenck's Dimensional Model of Personality and Gender," *Personality and Individual Differences* 26, no. 1 (1999): 5–11. See also Catholic Sisters Week, "Fact Sheet: Women Religious," accessed May 27, 2019, https://www.scls.org/wp-content/uploads/NCSW17-Fact-Sheet-on-Women-Religious.pdf.

[333] David A. Snowdon, "Aging and Alzheimer's Disease: Lessons from the Nun Study," *The Gerontologist* 37, no. 2 (1997): 150–156. See also Leslie J. Francis and Giuseppe Crea, "Happiness Matters: Exploring the Linkages between Personality, Personal Happiness, and Work-Related Psychological Health among Priests and Sisters in Italy," *Pastoral Psychology* 67 (2018): 17–32. See also Michel Poulain, "The Longevity of Nuns and Monks: A Gender Gap Issue Investigated with New Belgian Data," PAA San Francisco: Session 116, Experimental Studies on Human Morality, April 2012, accessed May 27, 2019, https://paa2012.princeton.edu/papers/122836.

Figure 7.3. Sisters of Notre Dame.

full analysis of their medical histories and records, testing and evaluation for cognitive capabilities, and a continuous review of their physical functions (see figure 7.3).[334]

The age continuum for the physical and neurological analysis of participants was 75 to 102 years. By these age ranges alone, an average of 85 years, the test group of nuns had anecdotally demonstrated a longevity that other occupations and groups cannot match. As each sister passed away, their brains were medically examined and evaluated for Alzheimer's pathology. A few striking results were evident early on. First, the sisters suffered far fewer Alzheimer's symptoms than the general population. Second, the cognitive portions of their brain centers appear to have been less impacted than others. Third, even when evidence of particular lesions demonstrating the

[334] Michael O. Garvey, "Screening and Discussion of 'Band of Sisters' to Be Held Feb. 21," *Notre Dame News*, February 18, 2013, accessed May 27, 2019, https://news.nd.edu/news/screening-and-discussion-of-band-of-sisters-a-film-by-nd-alumna-mary-fishman.

presence of Alzheimer's was present, their location and severity appeared to inflict less damage to cognition. The research demonstrated that the lifestyle of these sisters seemed conducive to minimizing neurological problems since so many of the test group continued into latter stages of their lives still functioning in teaching, library work, child counseling, and the like. Many in the test group, despite health problems, continued their work with children, caring and loving them sacrificially and, while displaying some of the physical symptoms that most would conclude to be proof of Alzheimer's, lived cognitively productive and lively existences. While the general population seemed to show the corrosive impacts of the disease, some of the nuns in the study were more "cognitively intact, with good short-term memory and excellent orientation."[335]

The results of the "Nun Study," which relied on diaries and notebooks completed by the nuns at earlier ages upon entry into the convent, manifest other conclusions regarding longevity and health. These autobiographical documents, created upon entry into the religious life, ask candidates to lay out their long-term ambitions predictive of the future to unfold. The correlation between positive emotions and a longer life could not be more demonstrable, and these findings are all the more compelling because of their durational quality, from the age of 22 when authoring, to each age of death, up to 102.[336]

[335] Snowdon, "Aging and Alzheimer's," 155; see also Elizabeth Eisenstadt Evans, "20 Years Later, Lessons on Aging from the 'Nun Study' Resonate Today," Global Sisters Report, *National Catholic Reporter*, July 12, 2021, accessed January 2, 2022, at https://www.globalsistersreport.org/news/news/news/20-years-later-lessons-aging-nun-study-resonate-today.

[336] Deborah D. Danner, David A. Snowdon, and Wallace V. Friesen, "Positive Emotions in Early Life and Longevity: Findings from

For those who possessed a positive outlook on life and its ultimate purpose, the length and quality of life followed throughout the lifetime. As a result, the more positively emotional sisters physically lived longer and happier lives.[337] While the "Nun Study," in its original form, narrowly examines neurological functioning when compared to general population results, other measures of physical health and longevity have been analyzed as well.[338]

In a longitudinal study on Belgian monks and nuns as compared to the general population, the percentage of religious members outliving their secular counterparts is quite significant.[339] Of course, social and behavioral scientists, despite the overwhelming evidence for a positive correlation between faith, religion, and physical health, often discount the spiritual dimension and instead argue that the social and communal setting of religious life fosters a healthy atmosphere that cuts down on life's usual stresses, while others argue that the rules and regulations of religious life cut back on life's usual vices, such as drinking and excessive behaviors. In religious groups where these behaviors are forbidden, the avoidance of their negative impact naturally leads to longevity. However, this explanation seems a bit quaint and less than scientific. Many believers drink, smoke, play cards, and even gamble and still live long lives. A counter to this conclusion might be that those who avoid these behaviors, and just as readily avoid the spiritual life, are not safe bets either. Religion and the spiritual life have an un-

---

the Nun Study," *Journal of Personality and Social Psychology* 80, no. 5 (2001): 804–813, accessed May 27, 2019, https://www.apa.org/pubs/journals/releases/psp805804.pdf.

[337] See ibid.

[338] Visit the Catholic Sisters Week website to see more of their stories at www.catholicsistersweek.org.

[339] Poulain, "Longevity."

deniable link to health and longevity, and there is "overwhelming research evidence that people can live longer if they actively engage in formal religious activities."[340] Study after study finds the linkage between longer lives, healthier lives, and religious belief. Some examples include the following:

- Church attendance on a weekly basis extends longevity[341]
- Church attendance by African American adults leads to lower mortality rates[342]
- Higher levels of religious practice lead to greater longevity[343]
- Higher levels of religious practice lead to lower levels of cancer, colitis, and heart disease[344]
- Higher levels of religious practice lead to lower levels of premature youth deaths due to risky behavior and violence[345]

[340] Moeller, "Religion."

[341] See Douglas Oman and Dwayne Reed, "Religion and Mortality among the Community-Dwelling Elderly," *American Journal of Public Health* 99, no. 10 (1998): 1471–1472.

[342] Christopher G. Ellison et al., "Religious Involvement and Mortality Risk among African American Adults," *Research on Aging* 22, no. 6 (November 2000): 651–652.

[343] Robert A. Hummer et al., "Religious Involvement and U.S. Adult Mortality," *Demography* 36, no. 2 (May 1999): 273–285; Johnson, *Objective*.

[344] Jeffrey S. Levin and Preston L. Schiller, "Is There a Religious Factor in Health?," *Journal of Religion and Health* 26, no. 1 (March 1987): 9–35; Yoichi Chida, Andrew Steptoe, and Lynda H. Powell, "Religiosity/Spirituality and Mortality," *Psychotherapy and Psychosomatics* 78, no. 2 (2009): 86, 88.

[345] John M. Wallace Jr. and Tyrone A. Forman, "Religion's Role in Promoting Health and Reducing Risk among American Youth," *Health Education and Behavior* 25, no. 6 (December 1998): 730–733.

The fervor and the sincerity of that faith reach their highest points when a person in health distress believes that a higher power might yet alter the scientific and medical outcome predicted. Those who have been terminally ill and then cured without ready explanation attest to the miraculous connection between personal health, healing, and the power of religion and belief. Not a day passes where doctors and medical specialists are not left scratching their heads for an explanation as to why this patient recovered while the remainder met their end under similar if not identical medical conditions.[346] A 2016 study noted higher percentages of people with a belief in divine intervention, including "74% of all adults agreeing that miracles of healing occur today and 59% saying that they or someone they know personally has been miraculously healed."[347] See figure 7.4.[348]

[346] For a fascinating empirical study of miracles on file in Vatican Archives, as assessed scientifically, see Shelley McKellar, "Making a Case for Medical Miracles," review of Jacalyn Duffin, *Medical Miracles: Doctors, Saints and Healing in the Modern World*, in *Canadian Medical Association Journal* 182, no. 6 (2010): 595–596, accessed May 27, 2019, https://www.ncbi.nlm.nih.gov/pmc/articles/PMC2845699/. See also Jacalyn Duffin, "Religion, Medicine and Miracles," *Interdisciplinary Encyclopedia of Religion and Science* (2009), accessed May 27, 2019, http://inters.org/religion-medicine-and-miracles.

[347] R. David Hayward et al., "Externalizing Religious Health Beliefs and Health and Well-Being Outcomes," *Journal of Behavioral Medicine* 39, no. 5 (2016): 888.

[348] See "The 70th Miracle: Lourdes Healing Officially Declared Supernatural," Catholic News Agency, February 12, 2018, accessed May 27, 2019, hhttps://www.catholicnewsagency.com/news/37743/the-70th-miracle-lourdes-healing-officially-declared-supernatural. For other inexplicable situations, see Robert J. Spitzer, "Contemporary Scientifically Validated Miracles Associated with Blessed

Figure 7.4. Lourdes, France, Where Many Seek Miraculous Intervention. Seventy Official Miracles Declared–One as Recent as a French Nun in February 2018.

At a minimum, many who hold fast to divine intercession in matters of health and cure may simultaneously hold firmer to a longer life than those who find a prayer for a miracle not worth the utterance. For those believing, the depth and breadth of the belief must naturally extend to a particular setting such as the prayer for recovery. A person of faith does not plead for God's help or a saint's intercession because of some superstitious hope for recovery or a better prognosis. Prayer humbly beseeches assistance because the devout individual believes someone is listening. Prayer for divine intercession assumes, very confidently, the power of divine forces in human existence. The nonbeliever is left to muddle in the exclusive world of labs and clinics, doctors and specialists, of whom there may be no real appeal beyond. In this way, the party nearing

Mary, Saints, and the Holy Eucharist," accessed May 27, 2019, https://www.magiscenter.com/wp-content/uploads/2017/09/Contemporary-Miracles.pdf.

death or suffering through painful health difficulties cannot be as consoled or contented as the party who believes this is part of his or her temporal journey. Indeed, in Christian tradition, this suffering should be welcome as a natural consequence in human life, a conclusion that bespeaks much about how our faith prepares us for the suffering and its maintenance. Long-suffering is actually a virtue, a human condition that is praiseworthy and good. The absolute avoidance of suffering would be not only impossible but also a delusional ambition.

At a minimum, having faith, belief, and a religious outlook prepares us to manage the suffering that comes to all and even, as a few studies have shown, "suppresses" the full force and effect of severe illness and terminal conditions.[349] The suppression should not be equated with denial but, rather, a management tactic in pain, illness, and suffering for anyone grinding it through difficult medical times. For the spiritual person, who deeply and unequivocally believes, faces these health challenges with the perpetual optimism that naturally envelops the believer—knowing that "this too shall pass" but also open to the possibility that a miracle might happen or that supernatural powers may alter or intervene in the natural world.[350]

No matter how you interpret this belief system, the party laboring under the press and stress of severe illness will be happier if their faith matters. Faith, belief, and healing even seem to extend to the afterlife as to the incorruptibility of the human body, a

[349] Hayward, "Externalizing," 887.

[350] Aristotle was fully aware that happiness is only truly achievable in the next life. See Robert C. Solomon, "Is There Happiness after Death?," *Philosophy* 51, no. 196 (1976): 189–193, accessed May 27, 2019, http://www.jstor.org/stable/3750216.

Figure 7.5. The Incorruptible Body of St. John Southworth in Westminster Cathedral, London.

scientific process of decomposition that seems halted in selected saintly cases. How otherwise can this be explained? If the laws of physics are altered, can the cause be anything but supernatural? See figure 7.5.[351]

Finally, physical health seems affected by an overall outlook on human ends and purposes. As both Aristotle and Aquinas have so often referenced, our final end is a metaphysical one rather than a physical one, for nothing in the body can be immortal. Indeed, those convinced of the higher order seem less fearful of the body's demise than those who see temporal existence as the fullness of our experiences. Put another way, if one is convinced that our death in a physical sense leads to another setting in a metaphysical way, to the Heaven we pray and hope for, then our physical turmoil matters less since it is a matter of time rather than the terminus. In this case, the human actor is happy even in the face of death

[351] "St. John Southworth," Catholic Answers Forums blog, accessed May 27, 2019, https://forums.catholic.com/t/today-we-celebrate-another-great-englishman/495014.

because true, blissful, and perpetual happiness is just around the corner. Religion, faith, and belief in a higher order tend to make us assured about our eventual destiny rather than frightened or deathly afraid.[352] A recent study on the possibility of divine intervention in health matters makes plain that belief involves "complex, multifaceted, and often multidirectional processes" that impact "key elements of human well-being."[353]

Aristotle

> Now if there is any gift of the gods to men, it is reasonable that happiness should be god-given, and most surely god-given of all human things inasmuch as it is the best.... For that which is the prize and end of excellence seems to be the best thing and something godlike and blessed.[354]

Aquinas

> On the contrary, the more one will be united to God the happier will one be. Now the measure of charity is the measure of one's union with God. Therefore the diversity of beatitude will be according to the difference of charity.[355]

[352] See Tufan Kıymaz, "Aristotle on the Naturalness of Death from Old Age," *Mediterranean Journal of Humanities* (2018), accessed May 27, 2019, https://philpapers.org/rec/KYMAOT.

[353] Hayward, "Externalizing," 894.

[354] *Nic. Ethics*, 1099b10–15.

[355] Aquinas, *Summa*, Supp., q. 93, art. 3.

Happiness, Emotional Well-Being, and Mental Health

In the matter of emotional well-being, religion, faith, and belief play more than a supportive role. In fact, according to most scholarly and applied literature, faith and belief are central tenets of being in a happy state. The "Nun Study" confirms this strong relationship between positive emotional bearings, religion and purpose, and a long and healthy life. The study found a "very strong association between positive emotional content in autobiographies written in early adulthood and longevity 6 decades later."[356] The Pew Research Center's 2014 U.S. Religious Landscape Study paints a picture of how religiously driven people have more active and engaged lives than those without faith. The center summarizes the difference: "People who are highly religious are more engaged with their extended families, more likely to volunteer, more involved in their communities and generally happier with the way things are going in their lives."[357]

The center is quick to distinguish life's less-than-integral actions as to religious faith and, as a result, found little or insignificant differences in the following categories between those that believe and those that believe less:

- Exercise and diet
- Recycling
- Purchasing decisions
- Environmental contributions

[356] Danner, Snowdon, and Friesen, "Positive Emotions," 809.

[357] "Religion in Everyday Life," Pew Research Center, April 12, 2016, accessed May 27, 2019, https://www.pewforum.org/2016/04/12/religion-in-everyday-life/.

The Pew Center continued its cutting-edge research regarding religion, spirituality, and mental and physical health into 2020 because the correlation continues to be strong and corroborative.[358]

These examples highlight a prioritization that places faith in a less relevant position than other human action of more consequence. Faith, belief, and religious outlook matter most and appear distinctly more marked between believers and less-than-enthusiastic believers in these content areas:

- Family life
- Personal well-being
- Exercise of religious faith
- Volunteering and community integration
- Social and communal life

The priority evident here is that faith and human action intersect, not as some sort of intellectual exercise or political posture but as a willingness to imbue faith into every corner of human life that really matters. To pick just one category, whether one recycles cans or bottles matters less than the care and feeding of our children. In the practice of our faith on a day-to-day basis, the believer emphasizes elements and components that the nonbeliever or less-than-believing party does not, such as prayer, scriptural readings, attendance at religious services, and engaging in the charitable works of a religious institution. The differences are charted in figure 7.6.[359]

[358] David Masci, "Why We Studied the Possible Links between Religion and Happiness, Health and Civic Engagement," Pew Research Center, February 6, 2019, accessed January 2, 2022, at https://www.pewresearch.org/fact-tank/2019/02/06/why-we-studied-the-possible-links-between-religion-and-happiness-health-and-civic-engagement.

[359] Pew, "Religion in Everyday Life," 58.

Essentials of Christian identity

% who say ________ is "essential" to what being "Christian" or "Catholic" means to them

	Believing in God	Praying regularly	Reading Bible/other religious materials	Attending religious services	Helping in congregation	Resting on Sabbath
	%	%	%	%	%	%
Total	68	49	32	27	22	14
All Christians	86	63	42	35	28	18
Highly religious	97	89	70	61	47	28
Not highly religious	80	48	26	20	17	12
Evangelical Protestants	95	79	60	42	35	21
Highly religious	98	93	83	63	49	31
Not highly religious	91	65	38	21	20	11
Mainline Protestants	80	49	27	18	19	12
Highly religious	98	80	61	36	36	18
Not highly religious	74	39	17	13	14	10
Catholics	79	48	22	34	20	12
Highly religious	95	87	42	75	42	20
Not highly religious	74	35	16	22	13	9

Note: "Highly religious" respondents are defined as those who say they pray daily and attend religious services at least once a week. All other respondents are coded as "not highly religious." See topline for full question wording. Catholics were asked if items were "essential," "important but not essential" or "not important" to "what being Catholic means to you." All other Christians were asked if items were "essential," "important but not essential" or "not important" to "what being Christian means to you." The survey included too few interviews with those in other religious traditions – including members of the historically black Protestant tradition, Jews and religious "nones" – to permit analysis of highly religious and less religious subsamples within those traditions.

Figure 7.6. Essentials of Christian Identity, Part One.

Anyone who dares bet on which party is happier has high odds of winning since Pew also confirms that religiously motivated and faith-driven individuals are emotionally happier than their counterparts.

The same can also be deduced concerning particular and specific moral behaviors and decisions made in daily life. For those operating in faith and bona fide belief find the following acts more commendable and mandatory than those who are indifferent:

- Being honest
- Forgiving others
- Time with family

- Works of mercy
- Gratitude for blessings
- Living in virtue

Pew presents these results in figure 7.7.[360]

Essentials of Christian identity, continued

% who say ______ is "essential" to what being "Christian" or "Catholic" means to them

	Being honest at all times	Forgiving those who have wronged you	Committing to spend time with family	Not losing one's temper	Working to help poor/needy	Working to protect the environment	Buying from companies that pay a fair wage	Being grateful for what you have	Dressing modestly	Being healthy by eating right and exercising
	%	%	%	%	%	%	%	%	%	%
Total	65	61	48	31	47	26	16	67	22	18
All Christians	67	69	48	32	52	22	14	71	26	18
Highly religious	81	86	56	47	69	25	19	84	43	24
Not highly religious	60	59	43	24	43	21	11	63	17	15
Evangelical Protestants	76	81	52	38	53	20	12	78	36	21
Highly religious	84	91	55	49	66	22	14	84	48	25
Not highly religious	69	72	50	27	41	18	10	72	23	18
Mainline Protestants	60	63	41	26	51	25	12	65	14	13
Highly religious	80	87	54	40	72	26	20	87	28	12
Not highly religious	54	56	37	22	45	25	10	58	9	13
Catholics	57	55	47	24	45	19	15	64	20	14
Highly religious	71	76	56	42	70	28	34	84	40	21
Not highly religious	53	49	44	18	38	17	9	58	14	11

Note: "Highly religious" respondents are defined as those who say they pray daily and attend religious services at least once a week. All other respondents are coded as "not highly religious." See topline for full question wording. Catholics were asked if items were "essential," "important but not essential" or "not important" to "what being Catholic means to you." All other Christians were asked if items were "essential," "important but not essential" or "not important" to "what being Christian means to you." The survey included too few interviews with those in other religious traditions – including members of the historically black Protestant tradition, Jews and religious "nones" – to permit analysis of highly religious and less religious subsamples within those traditions.

Figure 7.7. Essentials of Christian Identity, Part Two.

One other observation worthy of note from figure 7.7 relates to the current obsessive mania on the matters of environment, minimum wage, corporate boycotting, and diet and exercise. Any fair reading of these results infers a lack of distinction or difference between those that believe and those that either believe or believe less. None of these issues rise to a moral dimension in which happiness depends, at least in the fullest sense of the term. No one

[360] Ibid., 59.

disputes that a healthy diet will make one "feel" better or increase some facet of the health quotient, or that contributions to climate change efforts make one feel a tinge of self-worth.

Even so, in the grand scheme of human happiness and personal contentment, the endless grinding ax of doom and gloom regarding food, climate, corporate greed, diet, and exercise can never really elevate the human person to happiness. In fact, the very opposite seems to be happening as the endless cacophony of catastrophe and apocalypse takes a preeminent position over matters of family, children, charity to others, and the like. In many ways we live in an age of misplaced priorities where the gods of Mother Earth and Animal Rights get more of our attention than the God of all creation. Environmental terrorists are now becoming more commonplace as they seek to rid the world of carbon emissions using extreme remedies.[361]

Those who choose to prioritize the less critical issues of the day, even though many would cringe at this characterization, have shackled themselves to endless misery and negativity. Stated another way, there is no real, meaningful, measurable happiness in the food you eat, the rights granted to a cat or dog, fuel standards on cars or trucks, or whether one loses twenty pounds of weight. All of these criteria deal with transitory realities rather than permanent, perpetual, and universal truths or conditions, the only locus for genuine happiness. When animal rights activists care more for a dog or cat to be put under at the local ASPCA than the third-trimester baby soon to be aborted, we encounter a crisis in moral justice and proportion. The sacredness and sanctity of

[361] "Most Wanted: Josephine Sunshine Overaker," Federal Bureau of Investigation, accessed May 27, 2019, https://www.fbi.gov/wanted/dt/josephine-sunshine-overaker.

Figure 7.8 Property Defaced and Minks Released at This Site in Protest. Courtesy of the FBI.

infant life, its care and nurturing, may lead to unfiltered happiness while saving a cat is at best an emotive step leading to very little happiness. See figure 7.8.

In so many ways, happiness eludes those who fail to target what really generates a joy-filled human life. It is no wonder there are such depressive states of being in our young people, as well as escalating suicide rates and a slavishness to drugs and pharmacological culture that is now becoming impossible to fully measure. Yet for those driven by faith, belief, and a religion that advances the human dignity of every person and properly prioritizes our purposes for being here in the first place, the race toward happiness has much better odds. For those disposed to faith and belief think constantly about what really should concern us day-to-day—family, community, personal development, and, most crucially, the God who fashioned us, the God who is the ultimate end leading to happiness.

Aristotle

Therefore the activity of God, which is transcendent in happiness, is contemplative; and that most akin to it among human activities is the greatest source of happiness.[362]

Aquinas

The ultimate end, then, must so entirely satisfy man's desire that there is nothing left for him to desire. It cannot be his ultimate end if something additional is required for his fulfillment.[363]

Studies and analyses on the relationship of happiness, mental health, and faith are not only common; their results are generally consistent and favorable to the relationships. Whatever group is assessed, whatever age, ethnicity, or gender evaluated, the positive force of a religious outlook and a belief system in the world of mental health is fairly indisputable. Some examples include the following:

- Attendance at religious services bolsters a positive mental health outlook.[364]
- Religious participation leads to higher levels of self-esteem.[365]

[362] *Nic. Ethics*, 1178b7.

[363] Aquinas, *Summa*, I–II, q. 1, art. 5, corp.

[364] Diane R. Brown and Lawrence E. Gary, "Religious Involvement and Health Status among African-American American Males," *Journal of the National Medical Association* 86, no. 11 (1994): 828; B. Beit-Hallami, "Psychology of Religion 1880–1939: The Rise and Fall of a Psychological Movement," *Journal of the History of the Behavioral Sciences* 10 (1974): 84–90.

[365] Johnson, *Objective*.

- Religious participation by teenagers and adolescents causes lower levels of depression.[366]
- Community religious services reduce depression levels when compared to solitary prayer.[367]
- African American adolescents who actively participate in religious service have lower levels of emotional distress.[368]
- Religious involvement and participation deter drug and alcohol usage and abuse.[369]

The positive implications for a faith-based life and a dedication to the supernatural order have communal implications as well. For communities blessed with a belief system tend to have less crime and suffer less from the scourge of illicit drugs.[370] Violent crime, homicide rates, and other forms of crime and deviance

[366] Christopher G. Ellison, John P. Bartkowski, and Kristin L. Anderson, "Are There Religious Variations in Domestic Violence?," *Journal of Family Issues* 20, no. 1 (January 1999): 87–113; Loyd S. Wright, Christopher J. Frose, and Stephen J. Wisecarver, "Church Attendance, Meaningfulness of Religion, and Depressive Symptomatology among Adolescents," *Journal of Youth and Adolescence* 22, no. 5 (October 1993): 559–568.

[367] Christopher G. Ellison, "Race, Religious Involvement, and Depressive Symptomatology in a Southeastern U.S. Community," *Social Science and Medicine* 40, no. 11 (June 1995): 1561–1572.

[368] Sung Joon Jang and Byron R. Johnson, "Explaining Religious Effects on Distress among African Americans," *Journal for the Scientific Study of Religion* 45, no. 2 (June 2004): 239–260.

[369] Vangie A. Foshee and Bryan R. Hollinger, "Maternal Religiosity, Adolescent Social Bonding, and Adolescent Alcohol Use," *Journal of Early Adolescence* 16, no. 4 (November 1996): 451–468; Johnson, *Objective*.

[370] Byron R. Johnson et al., "Escaping from the Crime of Inner Cities: Church Attendance and Religious Salience among Disadvantaged Youth," *Justice Quarterly* 17, no. 2 (June 2000): 377–391.

drop in relation to bona fide and heartfelt religiosity.[371] All of these findings signify a more positive mental health perspective, a more well-adjusted person at play and work in the community, and a citizen more likely to contribute rather than simply take from the collective. Another way of saying all of this is that people reliant upon the supernatural order, upon God and higher metaphysics, tend to have their ends screwed on better than those without any semblance of faith or belief. Believers are not only happier, but they tend to be more productive members of a community, they tend to be adherent to civil and criminal laws, and they manifest what it means to be a true citizen living with others. See figure 7.9.

A person with a strong faith-based purpose drives more confidently toward the appropriate goals and ends for a human life than the person who lacks clarity on what the end of life constitutes. "Theistic and spiritually based beliefs and behaviors have been demonstrated to consistently predict physical and mental health," with the "awareness of God and better psychological health" a clinically demonstrable reality.[372] As most studies conclude, the relationship between spirituality and individual happiness appears tethered to notions of something higher, something greater than self, "something numinous (i.e., deity, life force, etc.), which is beyond and/or greater than the individual."[373]

At every level and measure, having faith, a belief system, and a spiritual outlook promotes well-being and provides parameters for our emotions, passions, and appetites. The religiously driven

[371] Robert A. Hummer et al., "Religious Involvement and Adult Mortality in the United States: Review and Perspective," *Southern Medical Journal* 97, no. 12 (December 2004): 1244–1255; Johnson, "Escaping."

[372] Ryan and Francis, "Locus," 774.

[373] Ibid., 775. See also Francis and Crea, "Linkages."

Figure 7.9. Forming Consciences for Faithful Citizenship.

person tends to be less depressed due to their own sense of security and inner safety generated by the beliefs. One is never alone, desolate, isolated, and left to fend off the challenges of human life when one has faith in a higher power. Christianity and most faith-based systems encourage the complete integration of this earthly, day-to-day existence with the metaphysical dimension encompassing a God. Happiness naturally finds a more suitable home in this setting because happiness is "God-centered, God-glorifying and God-given."[374]

This belief system, in essence, is a form of protection—a security blanket that consoles and encourages the human actor to face life not as a drifting piece of flotsam on a sea of turbulent and temporal interaction but instead as a child of God—an image of the Creator and a reflection of God's goodness. While some may claim this

[374] David P. Murray, "Happiness: Science versus Scripture," *Puritan Reformed Journal* 10, no. 1 (2018): 206.

characterization to be more fairy tale than an actual state of being, the studies and the evidence make plain how powerful religion and the spiritual dimension are when confronting all aspects of human operation. A 2008 study analyzing more than one hundred scholarly studies on the relationship of positive mental health and the role of religion found the correlation confirmed in 92 percent of those studies.[375]

Similar results on the positive role of religion, even in settings more conducive to depression, in thwarting the onslaught of emotional difficulties, were discovered in a major ten-year study of adolescents growing up in a depressive environment. Religion, the spiritual life and faith, was an effective deterrent as the study concludes: "A high self-report rating of the importance of religion or spirituality may have a protective effect against recurrence of depression, particularly in adults with a history of parental depression."[376]

Even the very young appreciate the nexus between faith and happiness. In a large cross-country, cross-cultural, and religiously diverse sample of kindergarten children, the Tata Institute of Social Sciences in Mumbai, India, concluded prayer promotes and advances happiness in the very young. In prayer, the human person, in whatever denomination, leaps out of the physical body and entreats

[375] Rachel Elizabeth Dew et al., "Religion/Spirituality and Adolescent Psychiatric Symptoms: A Review," *Child Psychiatry and Human Development* 39, no. 4 (2008): 381–398.

[376] Lisa Miller et al., "Religiosity and Major Depression in Adults at High Risk: A Ten-Year Prospective Study," *American Journal of Psychiatry* 169, no. 1 (January 2012): 89–94, accessed May 27, 2019, https://ajp.psychiatryonline.org/doi/pdf/10.1176/appi.ajp.2011.10121823. The evidence overwhelmingly proves the correlation between faith and mental well-being.

a higher power to assist, for prayer "has been understood as an inward communion or conversation with a divine power."[377] Part of the aim of this study was to determine whether or not prayer leads to positive child development and, if so, whether prayer should be part of the educational pedagogy. A prayer lessons package was developed and tested in the sample group. The specific activities centered on three elements:

1. Thanking God for everything
2. Requesting God to continue the blessings
3. Praying for the good health, wellness, and well-being of parents, siblings, and friends[378]

The results of this study affirmed that prayer "had a positive effect on the happiness of kindergartners,"[379] and the researchers concluded that "there is a high correlation between learning the prayer lessons as developed and prescribed in the program and increased happiness."[380]

No matter the age or group, the power of prayer, faith, and belief, as well as the simple recognition of a higher power that oversees our lowlier status, leads to a happier state of human existence. It is not a complex formula, and given the provability and demonstrability of these arguments, one wonders why our educational bureaucracy expends so little energy on these questions, or why the courts continue, at every level of education, to

[377] Samta P. Pandya, "Prayer Lessons to Promote Happiness among Kindergarten School Children: A Cross-Country Experimental Study," *Religious Education* 113, no. 2 (February 2018): 216.

[378] See Mary Fairchild, "Six Simple Tips for Teaching Children to Pray," Learn Religions, accessed May 27, 2019, https://www.thoughtco.com/teaching-children-to-pray-700148.

[379] Pandya, "Kindergarten," 226.

[380] Ibid., 228.

squash or deny the right to prayer and religious expression in the educational setting, or why our prisons cannot see the correlation when these institutions suffer from recidivism rates of nearly 90 percent. In some sense, the avoidance or shirking of these results says much about our pride and scientific arrogance. Happiness, we have learned over and over again, is not a permanent state but surely an achievable one. If we target behaviors consistent with our natural makeup, we shall surely be happier; if we zero in on how crucial social and familial relationships are, we shall surely be happier; and if we prioritize things consistent with their overall importance, in matters of fame, fortune, and wealth, of the senses, the body, and pleasure, we shall surely be happier. Of all these variables tied to human happiness, none is more connected, correlated, and confirmed than the recognition of our true station and grounding in life—a creature made in the image of God. For in this judgment, we discover the ultimate end of human life—to be in communion and in the presence of God, imperfectly so yet in the midst of perfection.

Conclusion

It is nearly impossible to argue with the factual, empirical, and evidentiary support for the positive role of faith, belief, and religion in the life of any person. The science of religious influence is quite remarkable, for time and time again, the data demonstrate that faith and belief lead to greater physical longevity than nonbelief. In addition, religion, faith, and belief deliver a host of positive benefits since these faith communities are not guided by unbridled hedonism or the pleasure principle at any cost. People of faith act more moderately than those without any moral strictures. And in some cases, religious denominations forbid certain behaviors, which lessens eventual medical pathologies. However, the virtue basis of most modern faiths delivers a moral undergirding that minimizes substance and other forms of abuse. Hence, the role of faith, belief, and religion in physical health is highly significant, even to the point of proving nuns with Alzheimer's lesions lack the disease itself. The "Nun Study" made clear that not only do sisters live longer than the general population, but they do so with positive outlooks, optimism, and a productive human flourishing that ties itself to purpose, vocation, and selfless sacrifice. Those active in religious life and church attendance not only will be happier, but they will avoid risky behaviors, are less likely to abuse substances, suffer less depression and personal frustration, and in general grow up in a more stable and loving situation. Even when the situation is unstable, the role of religion in deterring harmful behaviors appears quite powerful.

The results relating to mental health and emotional outlook are just as compellingly positive. By its very nature, religion and faith force the believer to think beyond self and anticipate a higher order that has specific expectations for proper human behavior and productive living. Instead of producing a narcissistic, self-loving person, faith and belief cause the actor to venture outside of self into the dimension where God resides. The mere appreciation of someone other than self goes a long way to shaping a happier and more attuned citizen. For those who believe prioritize things very differently than those who lack belief in a higher power. Happiness is fully achievable for the believer because he or she will ultimately encounter God, who is the only meaningful, perpetual, and universal end capable of delivering that state of mind. The believer knows this better than the nonbeliever, for in the final analysis, the outlook of those that do not believe is nothing more than a trap without escape, a prison cell without any release, and a dull, dreary individualism that can never produce true freedom or happiness. The believer is released from every sort of emotional restriction and from the emotional shackles that come naturally to those who merely ask, "Is this all there is?" A person filled with faith and belief knows this state of affairs is merely the beginning of things, for this dimension is very, very temporary. In the afterlife, we shall encounter a happiness that cannot fade or lose its luster, a happiness that shall pierce our very essence, filling our hearts and our minds with the perfection that only God can provide and leaving them completely content forever after. As Jesus said, "These things I have spoken to you, that my joy may be in you, and your joy may be filled."[381]

Rules for a Happy Life

7.0: That Happiness Cannot Exist without Faith and Spiritual Belief

7.1: That Happiness and Its Ultimate End Rest in Faith and Belief in God

7.2: That Happiness Can Only Occur at the Divine Level Rather Than the Earthly Level

7.3: That Happiness Rooted in Faith and Belief Fosters Human Longevity and Greater Physical Health

7.4: That Happiness Set in Faith and Belief Delivers a More Optimistic Vision of Human Life and Highly Positive Levels of Emotional Health and Well-Being

7.5: That Happiness, in Its Purest and Most Unadulterated Form, Depends upon Faith

7.6: That Happiness Is Surely Lacking in Nonbelievers When Compared to Believers

[381] John 15:11.

7.7: That Happiness Can Never Reach Its Fruition When the Human Agent Sees the World as Godless
7.8: That Happiness Lacking Faith Has Higher Rates of Suicide and Depression, Early Deaths, and Decreased Longevity
7.9: That Happiness Grounded in Faith Believes in the Power of Prayer and Miracles
7.10: That Happiness with God Always Fulfills and Never Leaves Anyone Alone
7.11: That Happiness with God Leaves All Things Possible
7.12: That Happiness with God Prioritizes the Normal Stresses, Strains, and Sufferings in Human Life
7.13: That Happiness with God Reduces Addictive Behavior, Deviancy and Crime, Social Disorders, and Dysfunction.
7.14: That Happiness with God, unlike Fame, Power, Pleasure, Glory, and Bodily Feelings, Is Never Fleeting or Temporary but Is Forever Eternal

8

The Rules and Recipe for a Happy Life

After considering these many topics, all of which are related to happiness and the happy life in one form or another, it makes sense to catalog or fully delineate the "Rules for a Happy Life." Since the beginning pages of this work, I have sought to lay out the many challenges that all of us confront in the modern world and how this tug and tussle between what we know to be and what we know works is constantly undermined by a secular culture, at times utterly devoid of any moral compass. Everywhere we go in our daily lives, we are besieged by this almost barbaric ethical and moral malaise. But in this humble work, and fully accepting that not everyone will agree with what is posed, I make an effort to provide some rules for a happy existence. It is by no means a perfect formula, but my readers should bet that most of it will deliver levels of happiness one could never imagine. It is up to you to tackle the content, to make the tough and difficult decisions to abide by these suggestions, and to accept that what is written here, really nothing new under the sun, is the tried-and-true formula witnessed throughout most of human history.

Most critically, we have used Aristotle and Aquinas, intellectual and moral giants without much competition. These two towering figures—central to our intellectual and moral history, despite their vastly different experiences—see the world in strikingly similar ways. Their moral reasoning on the good life, the ultimate end of human existence, and the primordial purposes for why we are here in the first place could not be more similar. From the pagan of antiquity to the Angelic Doctor of Roman Catholicism, the path to happiness is laid out with extraordinary compatibility. For this reason alone, the recipe, the formula, the guide and rules for a happy life are worth your undivided attention. If anything, test the waters—see if it is true or not. I am betting on Aristotle and Aquinas: they have been right so often you cannot escape their wisdom.

Chapter 1: Rules for a Happy Life

1.0: Aristotle: Happiness is an activity of the soul in accordance with complete virtue.[382]

1.1: Aquinas: God is Happiness by His Essence: for He is happy not by acquisition or participation of something else but by His Essence.[383]

Testing the Rules

1. Identify a vice, a fault, or a negative trait you are honest about. For example, is there a food—like candy—that you have difficulty avoiding? Or are you bound and shackled to a cell phone? Test your capacity to withstand the temptation by not eating that food, by not watching that television show, or by not being enslaved by technology for just one day. At the end of twenty-four hours, write down how this decision impacts your outlook.

[382] *Nic. Ethics*, 1102a5–7.

[383] Aquinas, *Summa*, I–II, q. 3, art. 1, ad 1.

2. Ponder living in a world with no afterlife. What if this is all there is—nothing but the here and the now? How does an earthly or a temporal vision of human life influence your view of daily life?

Chapter 2: Rules for a Happy Life

2.0: That Happiness Is Unachievable in This World

2.1: That Happiness in This World Is Partial and Dependent on Choices

2.2: That Happiness Is Not Constant Exhilaration but a State of Contentment

2.3: That Happiness Depends on Virtue and the Virtuous Life

2.4: That Happiness Connects to Proper Goods and the End of Human Life

2.5: That Happiness Depends upon Human Flourishing and Development at the Highest Levels

2.6: That Happiness Resides in Our Ultimate End—God

Testing the Rules

1. Think about the last time you were identifiably happy—that is, a period of time in your life when you could easily and readily say you were happy. In your view, what events or conditions caused that happiness? Was it a period of long-term duration or a fleeting moment?

2. Compare periods in your life when there was total exhilaration—an almost frenetic happiness and joy that does not often come along. What events and conditions, what circumstances triggered this high level of positive energy? Is this a state you wish to be in permanently? How does being "content" differ, and if

you had to choose between exhilaration and contentment, which would you choose?

Chapter 3: Rules for a Happy Life

3.0: That Happiness Cannot Be Solely Derived from Money
3.1: That Happiness Cannot Be Solely Derived from Material Possessions
3.2: That Happiness Is Less Likely in Poverty, Deprivation, and Impoverishment
3.3: That Happiness Does Not Occur in Equal Distribution or Communal Sharing of Property
3.4: That Happiness in Matters of Wealth, Money, and Possessions Needs a Virtuous Disposition
3.5: That Happiness Depends on a Proper Balance of "Having" and "Giving"
3.6: That Happiness Depends on Private Ambition and Private Ownership Rather Than Collective Distribution
3.7: That Happiness Is Not Assured Even When the Economic Quality of Life Is Highly Prosperous
3.8: That Happiness and the Vice of Greed Are Utterly Incompatible
3.9: That Happiness and the Virtue of Charity Are Completely Compatible

Testing the Rules

1. Have you ever shopped or bought something, thinking that the purchase will lead to happiness? Have you ever craved some material good or possession so much that you had to buy it, thinking its ownership would be all you would ever need? Have you ever gone shopping and bought a bevy of material things and upon

returning home been let down or even left empty by those goods so intensely sought after?

2. Material possessions are clearly nice, but no amount of ownership and purchase can ever lead to happiness. What do people who have "everything" always want more of? Is there a threshold of having "stuff" that eventually leads to simply throwing away "stuff" to buy more "stuff"? Have you ever wondered why material possessions are so craved and thirsted for? Can these same material possessions ever lead to happiness when compared to nonmaterial ends and goods?

3. Consider giving the money you were going to expend on a material possession—something utterly unessential—to a reputable charity such as the Salvation Army, the Little Sisters of the Poor, or others dedicated to works of charity. Record your internal perspective when you do this. What is better, buying the yearned-for good or giving the money to a worthy charity?

Chapter 4: Rules for a Happy Life

4.0: That Happiness Does Not Arise from Fame and Notoriety
4.1: That Happiness, Which Seeks the Ultimate End, Is Often Diverted by Fame
4.2: That Happiness Is Eternal and Perpetual in God, While Fame Is Fleeting
4.3: That Happiness Is about Others While Fame Is about the Self
4.4: That Happiness Equates with Contentment While Fame Craves Status and More
4.5: That Happiness Keeps Proper Priorities While Fame Manifests Inordinate Attention

4.6: That Happiness and Fame Can Be Compatible If Engaged in Charitable Acts
4.7: That Happiness and Fame Are Balanced by the Virtuous Life
4.8: That Happiness and the Lust or Obsession for Power Are Incompatible
4.9: That Happiness and Power, If Used Justly, Can Complement One Another
4.10: That Happiness and Power Are Balanced by the Virtuous Life
4.11: That Happiness Is Undermined When Human Power Is All That Matters
4.12: That Happiness Is Impossible When Power Lacks God—the Ultimate End
4.13: That Happiness Cannot Exist in Power or Glory Alone Due to Its Temporary Condition

Testing the Rules

1. The idea of fame—of being famous and in the limelight of adulation—is very often witnessed in the human condition. Being famous, many conclude, will bring happiness and joy since the actor has achieved his or her goals or aspirations. Imagine being offered the chance at fame. Would you accept the notoriety and all the benefits both emotionally and monetarily that come with that fame? From another perspective, is there a way to keep one's balance and well-being while in a state of fame? In other words, can I be a famous actor, a singer or performer, politician or statesman, inventor or entrepreneurial CEO and still achieve meaningful and real happiness? Or is it better to reject fame and all its collateral damage that seems common to famous people?

2. Is it reasonable to argue that excessive adulation and fame may hinder one's relationship with God and a higher power? Does fame undermine the natural priorities for the human actor and elevate humanity over a higher, more divine power? Would it be possible to objectively see one's proper place in the universe of beings, from the highest to the lowest, while in a state of inordinate fame? If this be true, does it not undercut any real, meaningful chance at human happiness?

3. Is it fair to argue that our political class, especially at the federal level, in Congress, is more readily corrupted than ordinary people? Is this because of the power the members of that class wield? Is it accurate to conclude that power leads to blind ambition over a virtuous disposition? Finally, can it be said that the political lust for power often destroys the virtuous disposition, which in turn leads to a moral and ethical pollution we now take for granted?

Chapter 5: Rules for a Happy Life

5.0: That Happiness Cannot Be Discovered in the Body

5.1: That Happiness Cannot Be Achieved in Sensory Pleasure Alone

5.2: That Happiness and Pleasure, When Guided to Proper Goods and Ends, Are Suitable

5.3: That Happiness Depends on the Body, the Mind, and the Spirit of the Human Person

5.4: That Happiness, in Its Fullest and Most Complete State, is Grounded in the Spirit

5.5: That Happiness Seeks the Incorporeal in the Perfection and Beatific Vision of God

5.6: That Happiness and Sexuality, in the Proper Parameters of Marriage and Procreation, Are Compatible

5.7: That Happiness, Inordinate Sexual Lust, Promiscuity, and a Lack of Chastity Are Contrary States
5.8: That Happiness and Artificial, Cosmetic Manipulation of the Body Are Inconsistent Acts
5.9: That Happiness Cannot be Fostered or Nurtured by Drug Usage and Addictive Behavior
5.10: That Happiness Is Promoted by Living Naturally and in Accordance with Our Natures
5.11: That Happiness Arising from the Body Is Impossible Due to Its Corruptibility
5.12: That Happiness Is Rooted Not in Feelings or Appetites but in the Human Soul and Reason

Testing the Rules

1. The entertainment and commercial worlds continuously sell the idea that sexuality in and of itself will bring joy and happiness. Sexuality is being reduced to physical motion without a moral or ethical dimension—as if a series of movements without corresponding intimacy and morality in human relations. Is this sort of definition conducive to happiness? Can sexuality be strictly reduced to physical action? What happens when a person has sexual relations with a myriad of partners? Are there physical consequences? And emotional consequences? Does promiscuity tend to objectify the human person?

2. Given a choice between living artificially with pharmacological assistance and its promise of happiness and living a natural life with the hopes that such a life will induce contentment, which would you choose? Why would it be better to live naturally without drugs rather than artificially on drugs?

3. Many times, human beings will be confronted with choices—in marriage and relationships, children, jobs and occupations, schools and colleges, as well as in a host of other life-changing decisions. What is the best way to discern the proper decision?

- How I feel rather than how I think
- What I want rather than what I should have
- What I desire rather than what I reasonably need or wish for
- What gives me the greatest pleasure
- What reason instructs in accordance with my natural state

Chapter 6: Rules for a Happy Life

6.0: That Happiness Does Not Reside in Isolation from Others

6.1: That Happiness Is Discovered in a Social, Communal Framework

6.2: That Happiness and Loneliness Are Antagonistic to One Another

6.3: That Happiness without Friendship Is Impossible

6.4: That Happiness Requires Giving to Others—Whether in Family, Profession, or Religious Life

6.5: That Happiness at the Individual and Communal Level Depends upon Family

6.6: That Happiness Cultivated within the Traditional Family Is the Best Design for Its Participants

6.7: That Happiness Differs in Dysfunctional or Alternative Families

6.8: That Happiness for Children Correlates to a Mother and a Father

6.9: That Happiness and the Marital State/Matrimony Are Superior to Mere Cohabitation

6.10: That Happiness in the Future Is Often Falsely Guided by Cohabitation Decisions
6.11: That Happiness in Marriage Is Fostered by the Having of Children and Being Open to the Procreative Process
6.12: That Happiness in the Marital State Is Not Negatively Impacted by Children but Blessed by Them
6.13: That Happiness Is Negatively Impacted by Efforts to Control the Birth of Children
6.14: That Happiness and Communal Health Depend upon a Strong Family Unit

Testing the Rules

1. Is it proper to claim that our natural state, our essential being dictates what is proper to our human operations? Could it not be said that procreation, by way of illustration, is largely a universal trait or want? Where do you see the evidence of this natural inclination? And have efforts to control the birth of children, whether by birth control or abortion, led to greater happiness in children or the mothers experiencing these interventions? Finally, are marriages that purposely choose to avoid childbearing more happy or less happy?

2. From your own observations, is it easier to have family without mothers and fathers? Additionally, what are the by-products of divorce and family breakup? Should we be dismissive of effects these alterations cause? Do they not matter in the grand question of being happy? And do families—that grow and produce, propagate and conceive family members—provide a safer and more secure environment than a world without children? Finally, what impact does childlessness have on the greater communal good? Can countries thrive or even survive in childlessness?

Chapter 7: Rules for a Happy Life

7.0: That Happiness Cannot Exist without Faith and Spiritual Belief

7.1: That Happiness and Its Ultimate End Rest in Faith and Belief in God

7.2: That Happiness Can Only Occur at the Divine Level Rather Than the Earthly Level

7.3: That Happiness Rooted in Faith and Belief Fosters Human Longevity and Greater Physical Health

7.4: That Happiness Set in Faith and Belief Delivers a More Optimistic Vision of Human Life and Highly Positive Levels of Emotional Health and Well-Being

7.5: That Happiness, in Its Purest and Most Unadulterated Form, Depends upon Faith

7.6: That Happiness Is Surely Lacking in Nonbelievers When Compared to Believers

7.7: That Happiness Can Never Reach Its Fruition When the Human Agent Sees the World as Godless

7.8: That Happiness Lacking Faith Has Higher Rates of Suicide and Depression, Early Deaths, and Decreased Longevity

7.9: That Happiness Grounded in Faith Believes in the Power of Prayer and Miracles

7.10: That Happiness with God Always Fulfills and Never Leaves Anyone Alone

7.11: That Happiness with God Leaves All Things Possible

7.12: That Happiness with God Prioritizes the Normal Stresses, Strains, and Sufferings in Human Life

7.13: That Happiness with God Reduces Addictive Behavior, Deviancy and Crime, Social Disorders, and Dysfunction

7.14: That Happiness with God, unlike Fame, Power, Pleasure, Glory, and Bodily Feelings, Is Never Fleeting or Temporary but Is Forever Eternal

Testing the Rules

1. During tragedies, such as death and natural disaster, to whom do most people call out to for aid and comfort? Why does this happen? If one is an agnostic or atheist, where should intercession be sought? What other alternatives are there when seeking divine comfort? Can human beings ever provide this level of consolation and care?

2. How does a relationship with God or a higher power aid or assist with major human problems such as addiction, sin and perversion, and mental depression and illness, to name a few? If human beings were capable of conquering these and other challenges, would God or a spiritual life be necessary?

3. Assume there is no God—no afterlife, neither Heaven nor Hell. Assume upon death, there is nothing further but a corporeal decomposition. Assume that the end of life is the end of all things. How do these conclusions impact you? How would these findings influence your happiness quotient? Or would it matter if you were ever happy or that you simply muddled through existence awaiting the end of time?

4. Now assume the very opposite—that there is a God and an afterlife, that life goes on perpetually and eternally. Is it more likely than not that you shall be happy or happier? For if these things are true, a whole, brave new world awaits without limitation or boundary. Given these two choices, if you do not attend presently, go to church, temple, or synagogue and record your sense of being after attending.

About the Author

Dr. Charles P. Nemeth has spent the vast majority of his professional life in the study and practice of law and justice. Presently, Dr. Nemeth is Professor and Director of Criminal Justice—and Director of the Center for Criminal Justice, Law, and Ethics—at Franciscan University of Steubenville in Steubenville, Ohio. Prior to this, he was Chair and Professor of Security, Fire, and Emergency Management and Director of the Center of Private Security and Safety at John Jay College in New York City. Recently, Dr. Nemeth has been named Professor Emeritus.

He is a prolific writer, having published numerous texts and articles on law and justice throughout his impressive career. Aside from a wide array of texts on law, Dr. Nemeth has authored a series of philosophical works on Thomas Aquinas, including: *Aquinas on Crime* (St. Augustine's Press, 2010); *Aquinas in the Courtroom* (Praeger/Greenwood Press, 2001); *Aquinas and King: A Discourse on Civil Disobedience* (Carolina Academic Press, 2011) and *Cicero and Aquinas: A Comparative Study of Nature and the Natural Law* (Bloomsbury Publishing, 2018). In 2020, he released *Natural Law in the U.S. Supreme Court since Roe v. Wade* (Anthem Press, 2020). He has also served as chief editor to the peer-reviewed journal *The*

Homeland Security Review and presently serves as editor of a new production: *Natural Law and Justice.*

Dr. Nemeth has been an educator for more than forty years. He holds memberships in the New York, North Carolina, and Pennsylvania Bars. Dr. Nemeth was previously a chair at the State University of New York at Brockport and California University of Pennsylvania—one of Pennsylvania's fourteen state universities. He is a much-sought-after legal consultant for security companies and a recognized scholar on issues involving law, professional ethics and morality, and the impact of privatization on public justice models.

Dr. Nemeth resides in Pittsburgh, Pennsylvania, with his spouse, Jean Marie, together for fifty-one years and blessed with seven children, all of whom are accomplished personally and professionally.

Sophia Institute

Sophia Institute is a nonprofit institution that seeks to nurture the spiritual, moral, and cultural life of souls and to spread the gospel of Christ in conformity with the authentic teachings of the Roman Catholic Church.

Sophia Institute Press fulfills this mission by offering translations, reprints, and new publications that afford readers a rich source of the enduring wisdom of mankind.

Sophia Institute also operates the popular online resource CatholicExchange.com. *Catholic Exchange* provides world news from a Catholic perspective as well as daily devotionals and articles that will help readers to grow in holiness and live a life consistent with the teachings of the Church.

In 2013, Sophia Institute launched Sophia Institute for Teachers to renew and rebuild Catholic culture through service to Catholic education. With the goal of nurturing the spiritual, moral, and cultural life of souls, and an abiding respect for the role and work of teachers, we strive to provide materials and programs that are at once enlightening to the mind and ennobling to the heart; faithful and complete, as well as useful and practical.

Sophia Institute gratefully recognizes the Solidarity Association for preserving and encouraging the growth of our apostolate over the course of many years. Without their generous and timely support, this book would not be in your hands.

www.SophiaInstitute.com
www.CatholicExchange.com
www.SophiaInstituteforTeachers.org

Sophia Institute Press is a registered trademark of Sophia Institute.
Sophia Institute is a tax-exempt institution as defined by the
Internal Revenue Code, Section 501(c)(3). Tax ID 22-2548708.